AGING PARENTS

How to Understand and Help Them

Richard P. Johnson, Ph.D.

LIGUORI
PUBLICATIONS

One Liguori Drive
Liguori, Missouri 63057
(314) 464-2500

Imprimi Potest:
Stephen T. Palmer, C.SS.R.
Provincial, St. Louis Province
The Redemptorists

Imprimatur:
+ Edward J. O'Donnell
Vicar General, Archdiocese of St. Louis

ISBN 0-89243-272-1
Library of Congress Number: 87-82364
Cover Photo: Richard C. Finke

Table of Contents

Introduction

This book is divided into seven chapters. Chapter One deals with the question of how to honor your aging parent. Chapters Two, Three, and Four provide the general background knowledge that is so very important in understanding the needs of older persons. The next two chapters, Five and Six, focus on specific skills and specific competencies, i.e., "Now that I understand a little better the aging process, now that I am beginning to grasp my own part in relating to an aging parent, relative, or friend, how do I best honor him or her?" Finally, Chapter Seven looks at the time when death arrives and gently indicates how the act of grieving can extend the practice of honoring one's parent, even into eternity.

Experts in the field of gerontology urge us not to forget a very important fact: All older people are not alike. They tell us to imagine two groups of people in a large hall. Those on one side of the room are seventy-five years old, while those on the other side are twenty-five. If their age was the only fact you knew about these two groups, about which group could you make the most generalizations? The answer is: the younger group. The aging process makes people *more* unlike than they were when they were younger. The way people respond to life, how they handle "the slings and arrows of outrageous fortune," pushes them in separate directions. There is more heterogeneity, sharper distinctions, and more dissimilarities among an older population of people than in a younger population. Like the deepening of wrinkle lines, individual personality styles intensify with aging. Each older person is unique, a son or daughter of God unlike any other, and each requires a different style of care.

Since older persons cannot be categorized into one homogeneous group, this presents you, a primary caregiver, with a very challenging task. Your own parent, grandparent, relative, or friend is very much an individual — his or her genetic makeup, physical condition, personality, temperament, history, and view of life, is as different as night and day from other people of the same generation. Every word, gesture, sigh, frown, or smile is as characteristic of that person as his or her fingerprints. Now, admittedly, this book couldn't possibly deal with all of these large and small individual differences. All the same, my twelve-year experience in working in this field convinces me that much can be done. These pages were written to share these convictions with you. It is hoped that this book will help you look at your aging parent in a new, fresh way. Our goal is to help you achieve the best possible relationship with this person you love. But if success is to be realized in this important matter, you must not allow yourself to become overwhelmed in the process. This would help neither you nor your loved one.

Perhaps this is one reason why dealing with aging parents can be such a frustrating experience. Goodwill isn't enough. In the adult-child/aging-parent relationship there are new challenges at every turn. Each of these cannot be dealt with individually, but I hope to address the general themes that underlie all the concerns that you may have. In doing this I hope to provide the knowledge base necessary for you to deal more confidently with your aging parent. Knowledge combined with faith gives you the power to genuinely honor your aging parent . . . and yourself.

Clearly, there are no simple solutions. I wish I could guarantee that after reading this book you will be able to say, ''Now everything's going to be fine.'' That will not happen. Dealing with your aging parent could continue to be one of the most frustrating problems that you will ever encounter. Trying to do the ''right'' thing with your aging mom or dad can be like dealing with an adolescent son or daughter. In fact, built-in problems in the complex aging-parent relationship could mean that sometimes the frustration level is raised even higher than what it was or is with your teenager. But does that mean it is all hopeless? Obviously, you do not believe that; nor do I. By reading this book you are taking a very positive step. You are trying to help yourself and at the same time help your aging parent. It uplifts my heart to see how many eager adult children there are with one purpose in mind: to provide dedicated care to a loved one who is getting old. It's evident that what these devoted sons and daughters want most of all, despite all the difficulties, is to truly HONOR their aging father or mother, and that is a beautiful sight to see!

1

Honor Your Father and Your Mother

The Book of Exodus, chapter 20, verse 12, states the Fourth Commandment: "Honor your father and your mother, that you may have a long life in the land which the Lord, your God, is giving you." This is one of the best known commandments in the Christian and Jewish faiths and yet our understanding of it is frequently one-dimensional. That's not surprising. As youngsters, this commandment echoed through our minds as a central theme in our religious instruction. The basic message that came across was: to honor meant to obey. Period. If we obeyed our parents then we were honoring them. Of course, other aspects were mentioned, such as respect and love, but obedience was the main point. If we were obedient children we knew we were "good," we knew we were keeping the commandment.

At that early level of religious formation this approach made a lot of sense. We were instructed to demonstrate faith in our parents as the legitimate representatives of God for us in our lives right now. To our small minds our parents were indeed godlike, and our religious training served to strengthen this perception over and over.

Viewing our parents in this light also fit in nicely with the emotional, mental, and social development of our personality. Indeed, our faith in our parents provided the foundation of trust in ourselves and those around us necessary for healthy growth. Ultimately, our capacity to be intimate, i.e., to share our lives, our innermost thoughts, feelings, and values, the cornerstone of emotional health, is a direct developmental consequence of our faith in our parents. Without this faith, developed so early in life, we would find it most difficult — if not impossible — to find peace in our lives. We would be overcome with suspiciousness, fraught with fear, and ever vigilant to protect our fragile egos from the attacks we thought were bombarding us. Our first love relationships, those with our parents, created in us an emotional center which in large measure determined the degree to which we would be open to others. Whether we believe the world is a generally safe place where we can find comfort and satisfaction, or a place of hostility where we must fight our way through, depends to a large extent on the trust we, as very young children, developed in our parents or significant others.

Faith and trust in our parents then provided the crucial core of our emotional selves; a core which stands as the epicenter of our perceptions about ourselves and about the world in which we live. This core, of course, still lives and functions within us even though years have passed and we are now the adult children of aging and aged parents. Our parents, regardless of our age or their age, are still our parents; and we are still their children. And still the Fourth Commandment echoes through our minds: "Honor your father and your mother."

In practice, what does this mean now that we are adults? Should we continue to hold to a limited understanding of this commandment, that is, should we focus principally on *obeying* the wishes of our parents just as we did when we were youngsters? If we are to change our definition of "to honor," where do we make the necessary modifications? How do we honor our parents' wishes if we feel these desires run counter to their own well-being? Where is the boundary between their right to self-determination and our obligation to make prudent decisions regarding their health and welfare?

The Fourth Commandment

To get some help from the scriptural text itself, we turn to the scholarly *Interpreter's Bible* for clarification. There, perhaps to our surprise, we see that the original intent of the Fourth Commandment dealt precisely with our situation, that it had primarily the adult child in mind, that it was greatly concerned how he or she would provide care for a parent or other dependent who was feeling the ravages of time. Only secondarily did this precept treat the taken-for-granted notion that young children should obey their parents. The commandment was principally a warning against the heathen practice of abandoning the aged when they could no longer support and care for themselves. The ancient Israelites would have been acquainted with many examples of this barbarous custom. It was happening all the time in the surrounding societies. History tells us, however, that the practice wasn't limited to ancient peoples. Even into modern times certain cultures used this method of dealing with the aged or infirm, those who were unable "to keep up." Nor should we become smug ourselves, thinking we are beyond such uncivilized behavior. Isn't the idea of euthanasia, now being touted by some segments of our society, a direct descendant of this "heathen habit"?

Abandonment

The Book of Exodus didn't mince words in describing what abandonment meant to the elderly in those days: "They are not to be sent abroad to be eaten by beasts or to die of exposure." Times have changed, but not all that much. A modern dictionary's definition of abandonment is only slightly broader: " . . . to withdraw protection, support, or help" or to exercise "complete disinterest in the fate of." Today's acts of abandonment may be more subtle but they still fly in the face of the precept. Clearly, to abandon loved ones is an extreme form of dishonor. Like all violations of God's laws, it also dishonors those who do the abandoning. It separates the violators from the godliness which is supposed to be their biblical heritage, their part in the Covenant, that sacred contract whose obligations are spelled out in the Ten Commandments.

On the other hand, Saint Thomas Aquinas reminds us that when we are able "to honor" our parents it means we display a genuine piety toward them, we show a fidelity to our natural obligations and our duty to act in accord with the will of our heavenly Father. Honor is intimately connected with justice, righteousness, and peace because it upholds the solidarity of the family. We show honor to our parents by a willingness to share our gifts with them. These gifts are not just our material possessions but, even more so, high respect, esteem, and reverence. At the same time, honoring our parents in this way certainly doesn't connote a blind obedience to each and every whim they might express. Let's look at two examples.

Two Stories

Sue is a fifty-two-year-old mother of three girls, two of whom are now out of the home. She works full time and is a loving spouse to her husband, Harry. Her mother, Helen, now eighty years old, has lived alone in a housing unit since her husband (Sue's father) died ten years ago. Helen rarely goes outside except to go to the corner grocery store, a short distance she is quite capable of walking. Recently, however, Helen began to ask her daughter to do her grocery shopping for her. At first her request was for a few small items to "carry her over." Now she is asking Sue to do all her marketing for her. What should Sue do? Would it be more honorable to grant her mother's request, to refuse, or to take some middle ground between these two? How would Sue best honor her mother here?

Norman's eighty-five-year-old mother now lives with him after she fell and broke her hip three years ago. She had been quite helpful to Norman, himself a widower with grown children. She did the majority of the cooking and light housekeeping . . . at least until three months ago when she began to act strangely. Norman has found the gas range left on several times; her checkbook, which she formerly kept meticulously, is now in shambles; her personal hygiene has deteriorated, as has her attention to just about any detail. Norman wants his mother to see a doctor about these changes; she adamantly refuses. How is Norman to honor his mother in such a case?

If either Sue or Norman were to give in to the unhealthy wishes of her or his respective parent, each would be exercising a counterfeit honor. They would be overlooking the actual needs their parents are expressing, needs arising from the inevitable losses that accompany aging. At the same time it must be said that Sue and Norman, in doing what is right, will most likely evoke some very negative sentiments from their ailing parents.

Sanctions

The Book of Exodus backs up the Fourth Commandment with two strong sanctions, one positive and one negative. First, those who follow the commandment are given a promise: "that you may have a long life in the land" (21:17). To an agrarian society, land meant wealth. Those who were loyal to the directive could look forward to a long and resource-filled life. If the whole society abided by the commandment, everyone would be able to enjoy a peaceful and carefree existence, including the elderly. They, too, could be confident of continued care without fear of abandonment.

The negative sanction was: "Whoever curses his father or mother shall be put to death"(21:17). A version of this biblical death threat came over to America with the Puritans. In their "General Laws of Plymouth Colony" (1671) it was stated: "If a child above the age of sixteen shall curse or smite his natural father or mother he shall be put to death." It's not known whether this threat was actually ever carried out. However, it's interesting to note that even the authoritarian Puritans recognized that mitigating circumstances could negate this extreme punishment. First, the death penalty would not be imposed if it could be proven that the parents had been "unchristianly negligent" in the education of such children. Evidently children who had not been properly taught the Word of God weren't held responsible for their "heathen" behavior. Secondly, no death penalty would be imposed upon children who had been so provoked by extreme and cruel correction by their parents that the children were forced to "curse or smite" their parents in self-defense, "to preserve themselves from death or maiming."

Surely the relationship covered by the commandment is a two-way street. In our present culture it's unlikely that we will come across aged parents who are inflicting on their adult children physical death or maiming. However, it's not uncommon to discover parents who have so manipulated their adult children, or become so critical or demanding of them, that the adult children suffer near-fatal emotional or psychological wounds. This goes far beyond simple hurt feelings. It can be so severe that the "psychological child" in the person dies or is seriously maimed. As the Fourth Commandment admonishes adult children to honor their aging parents, so, too, the parents must honor the children. Moreover, all the people involved must honor themselves. It's the only way the divine precept can be fully lived. The Fourth Commandment has the preservation of family solidarity as its central purpose. This cannot be fulfilled if an individual "makes light of" or "takes away from" his or her own person or family in deference to the demands of an aging parent. In other words, is it possible to honor part of God's creation by dishonoring another part?

The Scale of Care for Aged Parents

I have devised the "Scale of Care for Aged Parents" in an effort to provide some guidelines for adult children so they can gauge the degree of honor (or dishonor) they give their aging parents and themselves. The scale is a 1-10 continuum which describes various styles of caring (or lack of caring).

The low numbers give little if any weight (honor) to the needs of your aging parent. The high numbers give little or no weight to your own needs as an individual and as a caregiver. Weights of 8, 9, and 10 will forfeit yourself to your aging parent. It is in the middle numbers where you find a balance between undercare and overcare. Neither of the two extremes is healthy; they represent positions where you are not honoring your father and mother.

SCALE OF CARE

1	2	3	4	5	6	7	8	9	10
VIOLENCE	NEGLECT	ANGER	SUPPORT	EMPATHY	SYMPATHY	OCCASIONAL OVERINVOLVEMENT	CONSISTENT OVERINVOLVEMENT	HEROIC OVERINVOLVEMENT	FUSION OF PERSONALITIES

1. *Violence and Active Abuse:* Violence in the form of physical, mental, or verbal abuse of the aged parent.

2. *Abandonment or Neglect:* The withdrawing of protection or support from the aged parent; the allowing of life-threatening situations to persist.

3. *Anger or Detachment:* The display of poorly concealed anger or deep irritation; or, on the other hand, the maintenance of an air of detachment or aloof coldness, the perfunctory fulfilling of an obligation with the minimal physical well-being of the aged parent the only concern.

4. *General Support:* Freely given support carried out with a guarded degree of warmth and respect (though with occasional feelings of having been manipulated); the showing of genuine concern for the emotional, physical, and spiritual well-being of the aged parent.

5. *Expressed Empathy and a Quality Relationship:* The ability to feel and to ''be with'' the aged parent in what he or she had experienced in the past and is experiencing now; the establishing of a healthy relationship where feelings can be freely expressed and received with nonjudgmental, mutual positive regard.

6. *Sympathy:* The experience of feeling sorry for the aged parent, regret that he or she is suffering the losses that come with aging.

7. *Occasional Overinvolvement:* Care characterized by periodic attempts to "do for" rather than "be with."

8. *Consistent Overinvolvement:* The regarding of the aged parent as an object of a series of tasks which must be performed.

9. *Heroic Overinvolvement:* Care characterized by sometimes frantic and desperate attempts to provide for every possible need and want of the aged parent; and, correspondingly, the increased dependence of the aged parent who is not allowed to function independently.

10. *Fusion of Personalities:* The practical elimination of the distinction between the adult child caregiver and the aged parent; the adult child's needs no longer carry weight in themselves; he/she has abandoned him/herself to the needs of the parent.

Personal Sharing Sheet

1. Describe a situation where you wanted to "honor" a request of your aging parent but at the same time you knew that this would not be in his/her best interest.
2. Did you ever find yourself in a situation where it looked like honoring your aging parent would mean dishonoring yourself and/or your family? Describe what you did.
3. Where do you place yourself on the "Scale of Care"? Describe why you rated yourself there.

2

Understanding the Needs of Your Aging Parents

We've all heard about the "generation gap." It usually refers to those differences in values, attitudes, and world view between parents (mostly in middle adulthood) and their children (mostly in their teens). But, as you know, this book is concerned with another "generation gap." It's the gap on the other side of the middle, the one that exists between those middle-aged parents of teens and their own aging parents. "Middle" is certainly the accurate word here. The people in this age group are indeed caught in the middle and they are getting it from both sides. They are trying to bring up their own kids — no easy task in today's world! — and at the same time trying to deal with the growing needs of their parents who are now beginning to feel the heavy hand of time.

Beleaguered Middle-aged

It will be worth our while to take a closer look at what's occurring in the lives of these beleaguered middle-aged people. Then we can contrast that with what's happening in the lives of their elderly parents.

Work

Let's start by asking about something that, by any reckoning, has taken up a considerable part of their life: their work, occupation, or career. What is the attitude of people in this middle-aged group with regard to work? At once we find some interesting differences between men and women. In general, the males are mostly involved in the maintenance stage of their career. They aren't as interested in climbing the ladder of success as they used to be. Or they might still be interested but realistically they've realized that where they are at this point is probably where they will stay for the rest of their career. If by age fifty they aren't president or CEO of the corporation, maybe they aren't going to be. This is not necessarily a negative awareness, but it does affect how they view themselves.

However, if we look at the middle-aged female, we see a somewhat different picture. She may well have been a homemaker most of her adult life. Or if that was not the case and she has held down an outside job for many years, chances are that her focus has still been very much on the home, on the bringing up of the family. But now that her children are growing up and leaving, she might be ready for a new approach to everything, including the workaday world.

Family Life

Certainly with regard to the family, the middle-aged couple is at a clear turning point. They have just concluded the launching pad phase of family life, i.e. getting the kids out; launching them into their lives and careers, helping them start independent lives and begin families of their own. All this has taken a tremendous amount of resources — financial, emotional, spiritual — to accomplish. It's not surprising that these dedicated parents are in a state of energy depletion and much in need of rest. Emotionally, these experiences might be labeled bittersweet, partly because of the empty-nest syndrome and partly because they are looking at themselves and the future in a new way. ''Now that the kids are gone, let's get reacquainted, you and I. We can re-bond ourselves here and really start putting energy into ourselves, once again getting to know each other as friends and confidantes." The potential is very high for renewal in the marriage of a middle-aged couple.

Leisure

For the middle-aged couple, leisure has taken on a new face. Normally by this time in life they have arrived at an increased acceptance of self. This allows them a new sense of freedom to develop other areas of life than just family or career. "Making it" in the adult world is no longer of primary importance. The re-creating, re-energizing power of leisure time activities is recognized. Consequently, the desire to enrich this area of life increases.

Also, this is a serious stock-taking time. They are asking themselves: "Is our life turning out the way we wanted it?" From their new perspective, the idea of time itself seems to be undergoing significant changes. Since they are now seeing themselves as in the middle of their adult lives, they tend to measure time from both directions . . . how much has gone by already and how much is left. This provokes a sense of urgency in them.

Faith Life

Those who have studied the mid-life crisis tell us that a person of this age almost always begins to sense his or her own mortality more keenly than before. For many this could mean a deepening of faith. Increasing respect and reverence for things sacred as well as a widening of prayer life could be the next development. This renewal of faith can do much to strengthen resolve and give direction to the middle-aged person who now has a new appreciation of life itself and what might possibly be done with the important second half of this gift of life. Fruits of this new perspective can be peace of mind and a closer communion with God.

The Parents' Generation

After looking at the middle-aged group, let's take a look at the same life areas of their parents' generation. Starting with work or career, we see that retirement, the diminishing of physical strength, and other assorted effects of the passing of time have already introduced revolutionary currents into the life of a man or woman who is getting older. Sometimes this means that what were vocations before are now avocations, and vice versa. Oftentimes, too, it hurts when hard-won practical wisdom and priceless skills learned over a lifetime are shoved to the back of the shelf and ignored. Regarding the very vital areas of family and social life, it's mainly a story of drawing the circle closer and closer. The nest was long ago emptied. Children have moved away. Siblings and other relatives, old friends and business acquaintances, and many others their own age are going through similar experiences, or perhaps have already gone to their reward.

Final Stage

How do older people view themselves in this last stage of their life? They are probably, or at least they should be, going through a phase of their life called life review. We will get more into this important topic in Chapter Six of this book.

If there is anything that increases as we age it seems to be the amount of disposable time that is available. Frequently this time falls on a person who is failing in resources physically, emotionally, mentally, and financially, and therefore all of this time very often lacks direction. "What do I do with all of this time?" is a question many older persons ask. Nonetheless, the leisure life area remains for many older persons a place where they can feel useful and productive and consequently maintain their sense of self-esteem. Unfortunately, for other older persons it remains an unexplored territory. This can be especially true for men.

Spiritual Life

The spiritual life area has the potential of being a fantastic growth area for older persons. They can experience this growth if they are encouraged by their family to do so. You can encourage your aging parent through joint prayer, expressing your feelings of faith, and including your aging parent in your personal thoughts about how God works in your life.

Two Worlds Clash

We have two groups of people: On the one hand we have middle-aged children who are trying their best to do what's right for their parents and many times getting frustrated in that effort. On the other hand we have older people who are trying to live their lives and achieve the developmental tasks of their world. There are more things happening in an older person's life, more things to be addressed in each of the life areas than at any other time except at adolescence. These changes usually come at a time of failing resources. It is in this atmosphere that these two worlds clash, the world of the middle-aged child (or grandchild) and the world of the aging parent (or grandparent). Both groups find themselves in a period of depleted or eroded resources and both groups would rather not, if they had the choice, be faced with the hard decisions that they now encounter.

Three Stories

Described below are three typical stories about what happens when these two worlds come into contact.

The first story is about Janet and Bob and Bob's mother, Madaline. Bob's father died about ten years ago. Though widowed and alone (Bob was an only child), Madaline did quite well in her own home until last year when she suffered a heart attack. Since then she has had to sharply curtail her activities, requiring the services of home health care and Meals-on-Wheels. Her physical disability also seemed to bring about a radical change in how she viewed herself. Formerly capable and self-reliant, Madaline became intermittently depressed, and her confidence all but vanished. It appeared that she was incapable of making even the smallest decision by herself. Janet's phone would ring constantly with requests for Bob to do this or that. Madaline wasn't interested in talking with her daughter-in-law. She was always asking, even demanding, that her son "be there." At first Janet was understanding and even compassionate toward her mother-in-law who had suffered so much. And it was true that Bob was gone quite a bit. However, over time Janet's initial concern hardened into indifference and even anger. As the requests increased, Bob himself, devoted son that he was, felt more and more guilty about his own rising feelings of impatience at his mother's ever-increasing demands.

The next story is about Rich and Arlene. From his earliest days, Rich's father was everything to him. In the boy's eyes there was nothing his dad could not do. To put it mildly, Rich grew up with a very idealized view of his father. Flattered by this adulation, his father not only didn't discourage it but actually did various things to perpetuate this myth. One of the ways he did this was by always criticizing his son. "Rich, you're not doing that right, you don't know how to do things." Even with this constant criticism, Rich continued to idolize his father. Apparently his own poor self-image was drawing strength from the older man's self-assurance and swagger. Meanwhile, Rich's wife, Arlene, realized that this relationship between her husband, now a grown man, and his dominating father was not very healthy, but she didn't know what to do about it.

As the biological clock ticked on, Rich's father began to feel the effect of the years. First there was a series of minor automobile accidents. Typically, Rich blamed the other drivers. But then there were other incidents (some potentially very serious) marked by forgetfulness, confusion, or undeniably strange behavior on the part of his father. Even so, Rich wouldn't admit that his "invincible" father was becoming senile. But reality would have its way. The old man's health, stamina, and mental acuity were rapidly disintegrating. What could Rich do? He didn't know how to communicate with his father because he had never developed a quality emotional relationship with him. There had been no effort to establish an honest, adult-to-adult friendship. In time, his father was forced to enter a nursing home. When Rich went to visit his father, what were those visits like? All they seemed to do was make matters worse. To see his father this way devastated Rich and increased his depression. And why did he feel such guilt? Why did it seem that it was *his* fault that his father was becoming just a shadow of the man he used to be?

The final story is about Kay and Steve. Kay is a talented, energetic woman with an outgoing personality. She and Steve have no children. But Kay does have an eighty-three-year-old father and an eighty-year-old mother who has Alzheimer's disease. One reason this old couple are still managing to live in their own home is because Kay does so much for them. She goes there every day, cooks their meals, does the shopping, makes sure they take their medicines, and sees to a thousand other things as the needs arise. Up till now, the strain of what she is doing has not had profoundly negative effects upon her. Yet the signs and symptoms of the overburden are beginning to show. There are only twenty-four hours in each day. Her relationship with her husband is being neglected. Her own personal needs have long been bypassed. The duty, loyalty, and drive to do for her parents in the later stages of their lives is so strong in Kay that it keeps her performing at this very high level. But it cannot go on much longer. The cracks are beginning to appear. We can only hope that as her parents require more and more care she will know where to draw the boundary beyond which she cannot go.

The principal themes in each of these three stories (with some overlapping) are: (1) Janet and Bob's story pointed out how the *dependence* of Bob's mother, Madaline, kept getting worse and how this affected Janet and Bob; (2) Arlene and Rich's story emphasized the one-sided relationship of Rich to his father and how this produced *depression and guilt* in Rich when his idolized father began to show the effects of aging; and (3) Steve and Kay's story was a tale of almost heroic *overcommitment* and the strain this put on all concerned.

Physical Needs

Like every human being, older persons have needs that fall into two general categories: physical or material needs and emotional, psychosocial, or spiritual needs. Anything that we can see, taste, hear, smell, or touch is a physical or material need. When any of these things become necessary for maintaining life and are lacking, then, obviously, there is a physical need that demands prompt attention. Should these needs not be met by the older person's family, oftentimes the community will step in — hence the various social programs of the city, county, or federal governments. Specific examples are Meals-on-Wheels, housing for the elderly, heat and utilities allotment programs, transportation programs, nutrition sites, and a number of other programs designed for specialized physical needs. Caregivers should be aware of the nature and scope of these community services.

Emotional Needs

There are also the emotional, psychological, social, and spiritual needs of older persons. For simplicity we will classify all of these as emotional. Are they very important? Recently a number of influential research studies asked the basic question: "What are the total needs of older persons?" In study after study, right down the line, older persons themselves told researchers that their most pressing needs are not so much physical as emotional. Let's look at some of the most frequently mentioned emotional needs of older persons.

Need #1: *A sense of self-worth*. A sense that I am a human being and that I possess a dignity that deserves respect. Perhaps the idea of a good self-image can best be understood by contrast. What happens when, for whatever reason, a person doesn't have this solid foundation on which to build his or her life? It usually means one of two things, and both of them are unhealthy ways to age. The first is exemplified by people who look at their life and say: "My life has not been good . . . and it's MY fault." These old people have a lot of anger inside and it is all directed back toward themselves. Experts tell us that this turned-in anger is the root cause of a very serious sickness: depression. At any time of life it's a very unhappy state to be in. To spend one's last years in the private hell of depression is particularly sad.

The second group of persons who age in an unhealthy way are those who look back at their life and say, "My life has not been good . . . and it's YOUR fault." What happens when these people age? Again, there's a great deal of anger boiling inside, but this time it's aimed at others (including their adult children), at the world, at life in general, and even at God. No wonder it's very difficult to deal with these people. We speak of them as "cantankerous," which is another way of saying "There's no pleasing them, no matter what." It would be hard to imagine anyone more miserable. Persons in both of these groups base their thinking upon the same fallacy . . . they think they're not worth anything, they're unaware of their intrinsic dignity, and, saddest of all, they don't realize that forgiveness and healing are possible because they've been purchased by the Blood of Christ.

Need #2: *At least one close friend.* This is a central psychosocial need of everyone and especially of older persons. Many research projects have found that the healthiest older people are those who have at least one close confidante. These fortunate people have someone to whom they can go, someone with whom they feel perfectly comfortable, someone to whom they can tell anything — their innermost thoughts, feelings, attitudes, desires, etc., even their so-called "crazy" ideas. Perhaps years before, many older people had just such a confidante in the form of a spouse, friend, or relative. Now this good "friend in need" has been lost to them in death and is greatly missed.

Need #3: *To feel productive.* The need of feeling productive is an internal sense that "I have the capacity to do. I've done many worthwhile things in my life, overcome many difficulties. I can continue to do that now. I can keep going. I can run my own life." Or "If I can't run my life, I know where I can go realistically to get the help that I need."

Need #4: *To feel useful.* Feeling useful is not the same as the need expressed in #3, feeling productive (which is a *self*-affirmation). Feeling useful is an internal feeling that is generated from the stimulus of outside affirmation, i.e., "There are other people out there who perceive me as a productive and useful member of society, and this perception is recognized and appreciated by me."

Need #5: *To be treated as a unique individual.* To put it negatively, this is the need not to be categorized, not to become a victim of ageism. Ageism, like the other "isms," racism and sexism, is a destructive prejudice that exists in our society. Its target is any and all who are old. Ageism lumps all old people together in one group. Sometimes it's subtle and sometimes it isn't. It is composed of a whole fabric of half-truths, insinuations, and myths which pose as truth but are really put-downs of anyone with graying hair. Chapter Four will list some of the more common myths and show how they cannot stand up under the light of truth.

Need #6: *To possess a meaningful sense of belonging.* "I belong to a group to whom I can relate." Often the only group available to some older persons is their own immediate family. This is a deep need in all of us because we are social beings by nature. It's going to be present in us regardless of our age. Ordinarily, the number and variety of the relationships an older person can maintain are a good barometer of that person's emotional health.

Need #7: *To have control of decision making.* Free will, the ability to make decisions, is what sets humans apart from animals. This human gift of making decisions should not be denied anyone of any age except for the gravest reasons, i.e., the person is deranged or comatose. This means that sometimes we must allow people to make their own mistakes. "To err is human." Making a decision and creating a failure is actually a luxury. Successful decisions generate more successful decisions.

Need #8: *To overcome loneliness.* One of the most devastating emotional problems older persons are forced to face today is loneliness. Fast on the heels of loneliness is depression, the emotional "common cold" of our society, a sickness to which the elderly are particularly susceptible.

These are the primary emotional needs of older persons. Neither older persons nor you have the option of addressing these needs or not. They are going to be there whether you like it or not. But it's the thesis of this book that something can be done. Understanding these needs can help you form appropriate attitudes about them and design strategies to deal with them.

Critical Losses

Losses come into everyone's life. Enumerated below are the eight most common losses experienced by older people. This list is by no means exhaustive. Think of your own aging relative and identify his or her own personal losses.

1. *Loss of spouse, friends, or family to death.* Very meaningful, perhaps the most meaningful, and hence the most devastating loss anyone can endure.

2. *Loss of physical mobility.* "I used to be able to walk up to the corner store without batting an eye, but I can't do that anymore"; "I need this cane or this walker or this wheelchair"; or "My doctor says I shouldn't drive anymore!" Devastating!

3. *Loss of financial security* of a regular and adequate income: "I used to have financial resources, and I knew that next week there would be more coming in. Now I don't have that same sort of security."

4. *Loss of status in the community.* "I was an active mother before, I did something productive, I therefore had status, a place in this community . . . what do I do now?" "I used to be a carpenter, a druggist, worked for the phone company, a teacher . . . I don't do that anymore. I've lost that status, I've lost that usefulness that my life once had."

5. *Loss of family ties* due to geographic estrangement: "Yes, I have four children, one lives in New York, another in Florida, one is in California, and the fourth in Minnesota."

6. *Loss of physical strength and health:* "You know, I used to be able to clean this downstairs in about two hours, now I work fifteen minutes and I'm just pooped" or "I'm having trouble hearing" or "My vision is going."

7. *Loss of self-determination and control over one's own life.* It is common that older persons lose their ability to make decisions or at least for that ability to significantly erode. Their decision-making ability can be taken away from them by well-meaning caregivers or they can lose their mental acuity rendering them incapable of decision making. In either event they don't have discretionary control anymore. This loss combined with some of the other losses all add up to a diminished sense of self-determination: "I'm no longer the master of my own life the way I used to be."

8. *Loss of self-confidence.* Self-confidence increases as faith in one's ability to perform increases. Conversely, older persons often report their self-confidence has eroded as a consequence of the other losses they have experienced and they become at risk of losing their personal integrity. Statements similar to these are common: "I don't have the same confidence I formerly had, I don't have the same self-esteem that I formerly got from performing all the roles I used to perform." "There is something missing within me, I have lost my sense of direction."

Primary Task

Adapting to the multiple losses of aging is the primary developmental task that older people must face. Younger caregivers cannot buffer them from these experiences as much as they might want to. They cannot prevent older adults from suffering these losses. They, too, will suffer these losses someday; it's part of living on this planet, a part no one can control.

It is easier to handle losses in younger years than in older years. The experiences of older persons are significantly different in that they are irrevocable. They are living their last life phase. Younger persons think they can always do things "later." For older persons, this is "later." A loss experienced by an older person, then, is a much more emotionally upsetting event than the same loss would be for a younger person. You can't focus on these losses, you can't reverse them or take them away. You can't bring spouses back, restore mobility, or provide financial security. So what is there left to do? How do you, as a concerned and loving caregiver, keep your own composure and not be so overcome with false guilt that you feel that your own life is being controlled? You can only deal, not with the losses themselves (because those losses are part of living) but with the reactions, the emotional responses that older persons give to these losses. Let's take a look at some of the more common emotional reactions to loss.

Have you ever seen an older person who was anxious? fearful or frightened? angry or even enraged? Have you seen one who was confused, disoriented, maybe not knowing where he or she was? Have you ever seen older persons withdraw into themselves, get depressed, or become paranoid? These are some of the common emotional reactions to loss. Of course, these reactions are not unique to older persons. If you experienced the kind of losses just listed, how would you feel? In Chapter Six we will cover the topic of communication in detail.

Defense Mechanisms

Not only do older persons have emotional reactions to loss, but they also use psychological devices called defense mechanisms. A defense mechanism is an unconscious technique. Its purpose is to protect the psychological ego from being overwhelmed. All negative emotional responses (like anger, fear, paranoia, depression, hatred, jealousy, guilt) are very unpleasant for anyone, older persons included. At times these can become so intense they threaten the very safety and security of the individual. Defense mechanisms are invoked to prevent the ego's integrity from shattering under the pressure of these intense, negative emotions. Older persons may have an even greater need for defense mechanisms because the losses they experience leave them more vulnerable. Common defense mechanisms used by older persons are:

1. *Denial:* "I'll act like this didn't happen." Sometimes older persons who lost their spouse still set the table for him or her, still keep the deceased spouse's clothes in the closet, or still keep the room as it was when the deceased spouse was alive. This mild form of denial is almost like saying it didn't happen. It could be a quite healthy way of acting in a given set of circumstances. It might be psychologically risky to take this behavior away from an older person, especially during a period of intense grieving. However, if this type of denial persists too long, some concern should be shown.

2. *Total repression:* "It never did happen!" In working with older people we sometimes find that an event has happened in his or her life, usually when the person was much younger, but he or she now has no recollection that it happened at all. It's a kind of selective amnesia. "It didn't happen!" You know it happened but the older person will not admit it happened. For people who use this defense mechanism, this specific memory is actually dropped from their conscious mind. It is repressed so deeply into the subconscious that it simply doesn't exist anymore. These people, therefore, are not trying to be contrary. The painful memory has been erased. An example would be a widow denying the fact of her husband's death. "My husband is away on a business trip." When repression is this extreme it has become pathological. In such a situation, professional counseling is urgently recommended.

3. *Projection:* "Not me, but you." Projection is one of the most frequently observed defense mechanisms. You are having trouble liking someone at a particular time, but you know you are expected to love that person (for example, your mother). To protect yourself, you project your ill feeling onto her and say, "I love this person, but that person doesn't love me!" Older persons frequently use projection to salve intensely negative feelings. An aging mother might be heard to say, "I don't know why my daughter doesn't care for me, what did I ever do to her?" These uncomfortable feelings are not part of her conscious awareness. There may be a hidden sense of jealousy because she envies her daughter's youth, vitality, and productivity. There may be feelings of guilt

that she wasn't the mother she wanted to be to her children. She has chosen this behavior to protect herself from a frightening constellation of feelings which threaten to undermine her sanity.

4. *Fixation:* "I'm comfortably stuck." There are some older persons who refuse to act their age. They will dress as though they were fifteen years younger, modifying their appearance and their behavior to match the illusion. They will do this far beyond the degree which could be considered normal. They are saying: "I don't want to get old and therefore I will refuse to act like I am old."

5. *Regression:* "It was better back then." "When I was thirty-five, things were better than they are now when I am seventy-five." Older persons using regression will try to live in the past, in the "good old days." They will try to recapture yesterday. Mentally and emotionally they are not living in the present. They find it easy to fantasize, their reminiscing becomes stilted and myopically focused on life as it was years ago.

Having a knowledge of these commonly used defense mechanisms can help you understand the strange or confusing behavior, attitudes, or thinking your aging parent may show from time to time.

Two Care Principles

The first care principle is to understand the real needs of your aging parent and to clearly separate these needs from all other desires or wants he or she may request. Unless this is done, you could fall into the trap of fostering an increasing dependence in your aging parent. Doing this would be psychologically unhealthy for him or her and also emotionally overburdening for you. Therefore boundaries must be established, limits must be set, a realistic accounting of the amount of care, time, money, etc., you can devote to your aging parent must be made. If you do not set these boundaries, you could end up causing lasting damage to you, your family, and your aging loved one. Once you understand what these needs (not wants) are, you can move ahead with increased confidence.

The second care principle is to build a quality rather than a quantity relationship with your aging parent. The word relationship here is most important. It takes two to form and maintain a relationship. There has to be a certain mutuality built in. Both parties need the nurturance that the other can give. Is it an adult quality relationship if one person does all the giving and the other all the receiving? No, such a relationship would not be balanced and equitable. You want a balanced, mature relationship with your aging parents. Sometimes these "one way" relationships are all that the circumstances allow, but that isn't the kind of mature relationship you want. Chapter Three will discuss what a quality adult-child/aging-parent relationship is and what it is not.

Personal Sharing Sheet

1. Is your aging parent/relative meeting his/her emotional needs? How? To what degree are you involved in each need?
   a. A sense of self-worth
   b. At least one close friend
   c. A feeling of being capable and productive
   d. A feeling of being useful
   e. A sense of being treated as a unique person
   f. A sense of belonging
   g. A sense of control in decision making
   h. A method of overcoming loneliness
2. What losses has your aging parent experienced?
3. What are his/her emotional reactions to these losses?
4. What defense mechanisms does your aging parent use? How?

3

How to Foster a Quality Relationship With Your Aging Parents

Lynn's Story

This is the story of Lynn and how her relationship with her parents fell apart. For years Lynn's mom and dad lived ten miles from where she and her husband, Tom, were raising their three children, ages twenty-two, nineteen, and sixteen. The two older boys had already moved out of the home. The teenage daughter, Betsy, had been suspended from high school once and was currently "running around with the wrong crowd."

Meanwhile, a new complication entered Lynn's life. Her mother fell and broke her hip. Since her mom was going to be in the hospital for three weeks, Lynn invited her dad to move in with them. He had always been a domineering type of fellow with strong chauvinistic leanings. This was quite evident ten years earlier when he retired. At that time he could easily have lent a hand around the house but he chose not to. After all, household chores were "women's work." This underlying macho attitude of her father surfaced for Lynn when her mom was discharged from the hospital. Her mother's doctor had given her strict orders not to do anything physical for several months. What was Lynn to do? She made a very natural mistake. She felt that she had to go over to her parents' house every day to do the cooking and cleaning that her mother had previously done. But Lynn's biggest mistake was still to come. After her mother had recovered and was able to function fairly well again, Lynn did not stop her daily visits. She continued her now ingrained ritual of providing on-the-spot service and companionship for her parents.

Deep down Lynn knew what she was doing wasn't good for herself, for her family, or even for her parents, but the truth took a while to dawn on her. She finally had to admit that she was caught in a dilemma that she herself had created. By this time her daughter Betsy was heading for real trouble. Tom, her normally good-natured husband, was becoming more irritable every day. Lynn was feeling used, resentful, and angry.

On the other hand, Mom and Dad rather liked what had happened. They continually praised her: "How wonderful, Lynn, that you are coming over to see us; we appreciate this so much." Her father was especially lavish with his praise of his daughter. Lynn had to admit she was pleased with this. In the past, she had seldom received affirmation from him.

Lynn was now locked into a continuous cycle of giving, giving, giving; a cycle that was becoming increasingly destructive to her personal life and to the lives of her family. What had gone wrong? Where were her two brothers and her one sister who lived in town? And, last but not least, what could she do to get herself out of this mess?

Overcommitment

It's easy to put a name on all this: overcommitment. It's by far the most common failing of adult children in their relationships with their aging parents.

But when Lynn realized what was happening, why wasn't she able to break away? Something deeply psychological was at work here. Unconsciously she was being driven in a near compulsive manner to acquire something long past. Lynn's dad had always been more critical than nurturing of her. She never felt that she was fully adequate, wholly worthy. Somehow it seemed like it was all *her* fault, so add a strong sense of guilt to the turmoil she was experiencing. She had married young and now, as a middle-aged woman, she was attempting to fill herself up with longed-for affection. Catering to every whim of her parents seemed to be the only way she could rid herself of this awful guilt. No wonder she fell into the trap and was having such a hard time getting out of it.

Why didn't Lynn's brothers and sisters shoulder some of the burden? The answer is obvious. What message did Lynn give to them when she said "Dad, come live with me in my house"? She was saying, "Dad is my turf; you can stay away." Was that the message she wanted to send? NO, not at all, but she continued sending similar messages all along. Her actions kept saying: "I will take care of our parents. You don't have to be involved in this." Her brothers and sister reacted naturally with the thought, "Let's leave well enough alone; Mom and Dad are being taken care of; why interfere?" All this, of course, had a dramatic impact on Lynn. She felt completely abandoned. She was becoming desperate. By this time the anger building up in her caused great pain, resentment, and the beginnings of a serious depression.

A Quality Relationship

How can Lynn get out of this situation? To answer this question we must take another look at something that was mentioned in Chapter Two, something called a "quality relationship." Perhaps we can understand what this is if we contrast it with a relationship that is characterized by "quantity" rather than "quality." A "quantity relationship" would be one where adult children are spending lots of time and energy "doing for" their aging parents. They are doing *many things* for their loved ones (hence the word "quantity").

On the other hand, a "quality relationship" is characterized not so much by "doing" many things as by "being with" the parent who is now experiencing the effects of old age. This means that a relationship of this type is characterized by a feeling of well-being, experienced both by the aging parent and by the adult child. There's a sense of independence on both sides no matter what the physical malady or incapacity may be. And always the focus is on the person involved rather than the problem. The give-and-take of this quality relationship strives for balance. It has a nondirective tone to it with a special accent on personal growth. We might ask, did Lynn enhance her father's personal growth by implying that he was not capable of taking care of himself? How different things might have been if Lynn had asked, "Dad, what do you think we should do about your living here alone when Mom is in the hospital?" Even better would have been, "Dad, what do you think *you* are going to do when Mom is in the hospital?" Aging parents are best honored by allowing them to tackle their own problems. It really wasn't Lynn's problem, but it was her *concern*.

What a Quality Relationship Is Not

Let's look at what a quality adult-child/aging-parent relationship is *not*. It is not like the small-child/adult-parent relationship we all experienced in our early years. Rather, both of the people in a quality relationship are adults. There is, or should be, an equality, a mutuality built into it. The style of a small-child/adult-parent relationship is extremely directive. It has to be. The goal is to train, guide, and form the little one so that he or she can develop a healthy self-image and thereby be able to handle the multiple relationships that will come in the future. Nor is this a relationship of equality. The parent is right in saying to the child, "I am the parent, I know better, you're the child, you do what I say." Is that the way we want to be toward our parents? No. Is that the way Lynn was toward her parents? Yes, she was.

Nor is the adult-child/aging-parent relationship like a supervisor/employee relationship. The goal of such a job-related relationship is productivity. "I am the supervisor, I tell you how to get things done." What happens between an adult child and an aging parent should not be like this. Your dad or mother is not your employee. Your relationship with him or her is not principally to get things done, even though things have to get done along the way. The style has to mirror the equality that should exist between two adults. Even if your parent is severely afflicted with Alzheimer's disease, your relationship still needs to be one of respect and equality.

Another familiar relationship is that of student to teacher. In most cases this is also very directive in style. "You will do this homework, you will hand it in tomorrow, and on Friday we are going to have a test." The goals are learning. Adult children are not teachers of their aging parents. Sometimes information has to be given. It should be imparted as directly and as clearly as possible. But the style of the classroom still doesn't fit the adult-child/aging-parent relationship.

A Helping Relationship

A quality relationship is meant to be a helping relationship. It can be that only if it is characterized by a number of those qualities that have been mentioned. It should be as nondirective as possible. In other words, you should not say things like, "You know, Dad, you ought to do this and if you don't I'm not going to come over anymore." A helping relationship means not imposing one's will on the other person. It is allowing him or her as much self-direction as possible. This might not be possible with severely sick people who are demented or who are suffering from an organic brain syndrome such as Alzheimer's or any other debilitating disorder. Even so, everyone's dignity must be respected.

Ideally, motivation for establishing and maintaining quality relationships comes from within. Doing things out of a sense of duty, or because of an undefined but very strong feeling of guilt is not what is needed. Even acting out of a desire to keep others from being disappointed is not a good basis for action. "I must go over, or they will be disappointed." Disappointment is sometimes unavoidable. It is the other person's own reaction. It cannot always be controlled or prevented. Sometimes all that can be done is to help the other person deal with it. Did Lynn do this? No, even though Lynn had the best intentions, she nonetheless failed to honor her aging parents. Instead she succeeded in making them more dependent.

What is a quality relationship? Let's look at a closely related question which was part of a study I conducted several years ago. The question was directed to experts in the area of gerontology and administrators of social service agencies nationwide. The question was: "What should our goals be in dealing with the needs of older persons?" Thousands of suggestions came in. These are summarized here under seven headings.

Goals of a Quality Relationship

A quality relationship *fosters positive mental health* in your loved one. Positive mental health encompasses these five things: (1) emotional adjustment; (2) ability to make and keep friends; (3) ability to accept responsibility; (4) ability to maintain personal independence; and (5) calmness of action. Does your relationship with your parent fit into these categories?

A quality relationship *promotes personal effectiveness*. This means that your relationship helps your parent not only to survive but even to thrive. This suggests that the aging person is encouraged by your actions not only to maintain a positive self-image but even to be open to future growth.

A quality relationship *encourages decision making*. This means your relationship aids your aging mother or father in identifying and making personal decisions.

A quality relationship *expands the knowledge of the aging process*. The way you relate to your parent at this time provides basic knowledge about the physical, emotional, psychological, and social changes that are going on. Because all of us are novices at this business of aging, this information can be very helpful not only for the aging person but also for you, the caregiver.

A quality relationship *assists in problem resolution*. There are eight steps to this process: (1) Briefly state the decision you are thinking about making; (2) identify the specific problem; (3) define clearly the decision to be made; (4) scan your options; (5) assess the risks and costs of each option; (6) assess any personal conflicts in each option; (7) develop a workable plan or strategy;

and (8) make the critical decision, that is, solve the problem. To make any decision requires a "leap of faith."

A quality relationship *enhances behavioral change*. Change is what living is all about. This holds for the old just as much as for the young. It might even be more important for elderly people because the losses already experienced demand many changes if the necessary adaptations are to occur. But notice it says your relationship *enhances* the behavioral changes that your parents make; it does not make these changes for them. To be valid and enduring, the changes have to come from within themselves.

A quality relationship *promotes self-advocacy*. The "self" here is your aging loved one. This means that he or she is helped in identifying specific needs and in working toward ways of satisfying these needs. It does not mean that you say, "Dad (or Mom), I will satisfy your needs for you; I will become your friend; I will cook all your meals; I will come over every day; I will provide you companionship." It is not your fault that your loved ones are suffering the losses that naturally come with getting old. And if that is true, why is it somehow incumbent on you to move heaven and earth to satisfy your aging parents' every need?

What could Lynn have done to prevent falling into the trap of overcommitment? Planning would have helped greatly. As soon as her mother broke her hip, Lynn should have called a meeting of her siblings specifically to decide how the situation was to be handled. Together Lynn and her brothers and sister could have come up with the family's response. Certainly some siblings have better personalities to deal with Mom or Dad than others. But that doesn't mean that the full force of the responsibility for the aging loved one has to fall on them alone! "Let's do this together" is a much better approach. Decisions that are made without the benefit of all parties concerned generally backfire.

Characteristics of a Quality Relationship

We have said that a quality relationship has the characteristic of "being with" the aging parent. This "being with" doesn't mean that you are supposed to be physically present all the time. Listed here are three factors you want to keep in mind when trying to "be with'' your loved one in the right way. In other words, these are suggestions to help you establish a quality relationship.

Genuineness

Genuineness is the ability to share of yourself in a manner which is open, natural, sincere, and nondirective. What does that mean? First of all, it means to be authentic, to be who you really are, to be yourself. That includes being open and honest about your own needs. If you don't and look only at your parents' needs, you will, in the final analysis, be undermining the relationship itself. Was Lynn authentic? No, she looked at her own needs only to say, "Oh, they don't count; they are not part of me; that's not real." She was not allowing herself to be who she actually was. She was not allowing her parents or anybody else to realize the guilt and resentment she suffered inside.

There were other problems she was ignoring. She was very worried about her teenage daughter but didn't have the time or energy to attend to her now. Her husband was growing more distant, and she certainly had lost touch with herself. The goal of genuineness is mutual trust. You drop the pretenses and the defenses. When you can do that, your aging parents will be more likely to follow suit. Don't sell them short. Don't say, "Oh well, Dad never was honest with anybody," or "It's very difficult for Mom to show her feelings." Have you ever tested it out? Have you tried to understand their feelings? Or have you told them what your own feelings were? Maybe they would surprise you. Have you expressed yourself clearly, directly, and with authenticity? It is your obligation to do so.

As an example of a genuine response, let's rewrite the exchange between Lynn and her father. He says to her, "Lynn, aren't you coming over today? What will we do for lunch?" A genuine response on the part of Lynn might be something like this: "Dad, I know you and Mom would like me to come over today." She has acknowledged his needs. She continues: "I can't come over." Is that clear and direct? "I love you very much and I want the best for both of you. I want and need the independence to feel unencumbered by coming over every day. I want you and Mom to be as independent as possible also." Notice that all those sentences started with the word "I." She is not saying, "Dad, you don't need me today; you can fix your own lunch." Nor is she hiding herself in saying, "Gee, Dad, I can't come because I have to take Betsy to the doctor" or "I have other things to do." Those statements are not completely true. The truth is what? Lynn wants to be unencumbered by the situation; she wants a break, and she wants the same independence for her parents. Now Dad is probably going to retaliate and say, "What do you mean you are not coming over today? What is all this talk about independence?" But Lynn has done the right thing. She is being genuine. She is expressing clearly and directly her own feelings and her own thoughts. The word "you" is frequently accusatory. Start your genuine statements with the word "I" and you will receive more understanding and better results.

Empathy

Empathy is the second trait of a quality relationship. It is the ability of the adult child to recognize fully what the aging parent is communicating; understand where the aging parent "is" emotionally; and see the world as the aging parent sees it. Empathy is not to be confused with sympathy. Sympathy is used at wakes and funerals: "I am sorry for your trouble." Sympathy means that you take your own emotions and express them to the other person for that person's trouble. Empathy is trying to reflect back to that person what you think that person is feeling or thinking. You are basically restating the communication you have just received. You are not trying to solve anything; you are not trying to come to any kind of decision. You are simply saying that you understand what was just said to you. To feel really understood is a very comforting thing.

Let's look at an example of empathy, again using Lynn's story. Her mother says, "Lynn, you know your father is not one to do for himself. He needs your help. I wish I could do for him now but I can't." Lynn says, "I know how inadequate you feel since your fall and how hard it is for you to see all the things that Dad needs." Basically all Lynn said is what her mother had just said to her, "I know how inadequate you feel since your fall." There was some reading between the lines, of course. It's true, Lynn's mom has suffered certain losses since the fall. She is no longer mobile; she feels like she can't do all she used to; she feels inadequate. Lynn said to her, "I know how you feel, Mom." Then she follows that up by acknowledging that it's particularly distressing for her mom not to be able to fulfill all of Dad's needs. What is Mom's response going to be if Lynn said something like: "I know how inadequate you feel and I know it is hard for you not to be able to do for Dad like you used to"? Mom might well respond, "You are right, Lynn, it is hard." Lynn is "with" her mother; she is emotionally "there." The bond between Lynn and her mother is going to be stronger and her mother is going to think well of her daughter. Lynn is probably doing the best thing she can do for her mother. It's much more important than vacuuming the living room rug or fixing an egg salad sandwich.

Respect

Unconditional positive regard or respect is the third quality of this kind of relationship. It is an attitude which accepts the right of the aging parent to think and feel the way he or she wishes. It's saying in your mind to your aging parent: "Hey, it's okay. That's not the way I do things, but if you want to do things that way, that's fine with me. I am not going to make you live according to my standards because my standards are different than yours. I am going to let you know what my opinions or ideas are, but you are the master of your own universe. You do what you think is right." In this there is no hint of judgment, criticism, or disapproval. There is no arguing, threatening, ridiculing, rejecting, and be-littling. You give affirmation and acceptance.

Let's look at Lynn's story again and see how it could have exemplified respect. Her father says, "Lynn, you know you never come by the way you used to." That is clearly a loaded statement. What is being said? You better start coming over. Lynn could interpret this statement as a threat. She could say something back like, "You have no right to say that to me." I know some adult children who would say exactly that to their parents. "You have no right to say that to me, don't you know I have a life of my own? Don't you know I have things to do in my life? When you were my age you weren't encumbered by stuff like this." That adult child is going to walk out of that house and think, "My goodness, why did I say that; what am I doing? This is not the way I want to react to my parents; this is not the way I want to react to anybody; but I am doing it. This is crazy." Suppose Lynn would say something like, "It sounds like you want me to come over more often. I know that you feel I need to be there more often. I respect your position on that and I hope you can respect mine." Is that clear and direct? Yes. So many times our communications with our adult parents are muddled and hazy.

In the final analysis, our only goal with our aging parents is to love them. We honor them when we can love. But this love has to be shown. The road to expressed love is the road of a quality relationship. A quality relationship is not cheap or quick, it is not shallow, nor is it easy. It takes work! This chapter has provided you with a path to follow leading to a quality relationship. The path is rocky and hilly, but it leads to a land of honor . . . a land where peace and harmony prevail in an atmosphere made confident and bright by the light of the Spirit.

Personal Sharing Sheet

1. To what degree is your relationship with your aging parent/relative a "doing for" relationship rather than a "being with" relationship?
2. To what degree is your relationship with your aging parent/relative a . . .
   a. student-teacher relationship?
   b. employee-supervisor relationship?
   c. child-parent relationship?
3. What could you be doing now to HELP your aging parent . . .
   a. foster positive mental health?
   b. promote personal effectiveness?
   c. encourage decision making?

d. expand knowledge of the aging process?

e. assist in problem resolution?

f. enhance behavioral change?

g. promote self-advocacy?

4. Formulate a *genuine* response to your aging parent if he/she said to you . . .

"I want you and your brother (sister) to promise me that you will never put me in a nursing home."

5. Formulate an *empathic* response to your aging parent if he/she said to you . . .

"When your father (mother) was alive things like this never happened!"

6. Formulate a *respectful* response to your aging parent if he/she said to you . . .

"You never come by the way you used to."

4

Breaking Down Barriers Between You and Your Aging Parents

Your own personal attitude about aging in general, probably more than anything else, colors the way you deal with your aging parents. Because of that, this chapter opens with a little quiz. Its purpose is to bring to the surface some of the underlying assumptions and attitudes people have about aging. The following fourteen questions are to be answered with a simple "yes" or "no." Try to answer them with *all* older persons in mind, not just your own aging parents.

1. Are old people narrow-minded?
2. Do old people worry about unimportant things?
3. Do old people feel sorry for themselves?
4. Do old people live mainly in the past?
5. Are old people stubborn?
6. Is it true old people cannot manage their own affairs?
7. Are old people cranky and irritable?
8. Do old people like to be waited on?

9. Do old people feel depressed most of the time?
10. Are old people bad patients when they are ill?
11. Are old people boring?
12. Are old people untidy and careless about their appearance?
13. Is it true old people cannot concentrate even on simple tasks?
14. Are old people unable to acquire new knowledge?

Since you were asked to respond with either a "yes" or a "no," your answer probably reflected how you read the question at the moment. It's my opinion that for each of these questions "no" is closer to the truth than "yes." I say that for several reasons. First, the questions as written are too sweeping, too all-embracing. They seem to be asking about *all* old people and are accusing the whole group of possessing some unattractive trait or exhibiting some negative behavior *all the time*. We know that isn't true. Many people who are of advanced years by the calendar don't show this pattern at all. Moreover, all of these behaviors can be seen in some people who are decades away from "old age." None is the exclusive property of the elderly.

Aging: An Emotional Process

Another even more basic reason is that the questions imply that the particular trait or behavior is the result of the aging process itself. For example, question #7 suggests that an old person is cranky *because he or she is old*. The truth is, that person is cranky because something has happened to him or her. This something — probably one of the losses referred to in Chapter Three — has no intrinsic or direct connection with growing old. It can happen to anyone at any time. Whenever it happens, whether to young or old, it always provokes some emotional reaction. Your aging parents may exhibit crankiness, stubbornness, or any other of these negative traits. But, in any case, aging itself has not produced them. Some other event, situation, personal history, or physical process has been at work. And always, an emotion or strong feeling is involved. It is important to realize that aging is as much an emotional process as it is a physical one.

Intelligence and Aging

Let's look at #13 and #14 to see some of the implications of those questions. There has been a lot of research to indicate that older people have a lower intelligence level than younger persons. This has been proven to be a fallacy. This information was produced by cross-sectional studies. They went like this: In year A they took a group of seventy-five-year-old people and gave them an intelligence test. Next they gave the same intelligence test to an equal group of thirty-five-year-old people. What the researchers found was that the younger people scored higher than the older people. These results were published, picked up by the national media, and more quickly than you could say "false research," the world believed that intelligence declines with advancing age. This simply isn't so. The seventy-five-year-old people scored lower for two big reasons, neither of which had anything to do with intelligence. First, the number of years the average older person attended school was four and a half years less than the average thirty-five-year-old person. Secondly, people in the older group were forty years farther away from the formal education than the younger group. The intelligence tests given measured mastery of facts taught in formal education. No means to measure "life experience" has yet been devised.

Fortunately, that was not the only testing done in this area. More recent research has come up with the following: There are some areas of intelligence where older people decline very slowly. Their ability to recall quickly seems to decline after about age fifty, but only very, very slowly, imperceptibly slow. However, while intelligence can be measured in terms of productivity, it can also be measured in terms of exercising a level of caution. Older persons may not have to reinvent the wheel because they have experience. They already know how to do this or that. The safety record of older workers, for instance, is much better than the safety record of younger workers. These items are clear measures of intelligence. All things being equal, older persons are no less intelligent than are younger persons. Sometimes, unfortunately, we think they are because we've got some problems with understanding the aging process itself. But the problems are ours. We are holding onto some unfounded assumptions about "old age." We have to revise our stereotypic view of those we consider "over the hill." Unless we can do that, we will never be able to establish a healthy relationship with our own aged loved one.

Hillary's Story

Let's look at an example of an adult child who suffers from an attitudinal distortion about older persons. Hillary is a forty-eight-year-old woman who is active, fun-loving, and very pretty. She has always enjoyed herself and the people around her; she is fun to be with; she has always been the life of any party she has gone to. She plays racquetball weekly and jogs two miles every day. Hillary's mother was much the same as Hillary when she was younger. As a matter of fact, Hillary and her seventy-three-year-old mom have, in the past, enjoyed many active times together. However, over the past two years Hillary began avoiding her mom. They used to meet every week for lunch and have a long walk afterward. This became much more intermittent as Hillary's mom requested that the walks become shorter. Mom was slowing down, normally and naturally. When compared to most people her age, she was probably in better physical shape than most seventy-three year olds. Hillary's avoidance of her mom, however, was actually an attempt to escape or deny her own aging. She was unable to reconcile in her mind the idea of aging in its normal and natural consequences with the fact that her mother and eventually she, herself, would face these physical losses. Hillary didn't want to get older. Her attitude about aging, and especially the specter of her own aging, was distorted and consequently it was very dysfunctional for her as a daughter, and it was certainly damaging her relationship with her mother.

Myths and Stereotypes

There are other attitudinal problems that frequently interfere with healthy relationships. Sometimes called "myths" and sometimes called "stereotypes," they are often used interchangeably in popular literature. A myth is a false opinion or belief about something. A stereotype is a rigid, standardized perception about a category of people or things.

There are many examples of this type of thinking. Let's look at the case of Harry. Harry's father had just celebrated his sixty-fifth birthday and had retired from a thirty-year position the same week. Harry himself was busy climbing the ladder of success and, up to this point, would eagerly share his successes and his business triumphs with his dad. Somehow, after his father's retirement Harry seemed to change in the way that he related to his dad. Now the relationship had grown somewhat distant and strained. What had disturbed his formerly happy relationship with his father was a myth that Harry had "bought into" many years ago. Without being the slightest bit aware of what was going on, Harry had always harbored the idea, the myth, that men were only men if they worked, if they were somehow productive.

Sixty-five and Retirement

Sixty-five is our culture's normal retirement age; unfortunately, that's a myth in itself. This myth developed in 1873. Bismarck, who was then chancellor of the new Germany, took a look at all the graphs and charts on life longevity in Germany and realized that only about three percent of the people lived beyond their sixty-fifth year. Bismarck wanted to be looked upon as being a very forward looking leader so he instituted with great fanfare his equivalent of social security or pension welfare system. This was the first time that any government had ever done that. He knew if he graphed sixty-five as the time that people would start receiving benefits he'd be paying out very few benefits because, at that time, longevity was not much beyond that age. Today longevity is much more than that and yet we are stuck with sixty-five as the beginning of "old age."

This chronological marker is really very silly and potentially harmful because it may become a self-fulfilling prophecy for old persons. In any event, since sixty-five is our culture's normal retirement age, Harry equated that age with nonproductivity, nongrowth, and generally a self-depreciating kind of posture. Harry couldn't associate himself with such negativism. His own mythological and stereotypical ideas about retirement and about growing older and about the watershed age of sixty-five inhibited him from really enjoying the new-found lifestyle that his father was experiencing. This is a prime example of how myths and stereotypes can impair the way you relate to your aging parent.

Some persons have the idea that old age is a period of constant decline and decay. Very rarely do we look at some of the positive things that may come with aging: the wisdom, the experience, and the mellowness that can emerge in one's later years. In other cultures age is revered. In our culture we seem to do the opposite; somehow being young is seen as an accomplishment in itself. Why? Actually the opposite is true. How did we get that way?

No New Tricks

One prevalent myth is the idea that older people can't learn new things. As the saying goes: "You can't teach an old dog new tricks." Many of us have this statement working somewhere down deep and we may actually believe that it is true. To test this hypothesis, IBM did an interesting study. They identified a group of workers aged fifty-five and older whom they wanted to retrain. Then they compared this group to people they were retraining who were age thirty-five and under. Lo and behold, they found no differences in their ability to learn and to apply their learning. The educators who did the training reported the older people to be better students. They did their homework and paid better attention. That says something very positive about aging. People can improve at any age if they want to, provided they are surrounded by people who recognize that and encourage them. But if they are surrounded by people who believe all sorts of myths and stereotypes about the elderly, then older persons will not improve but become dependent. The most damaging thing about myths and stereotypes is precisely that: older people themselves start believing them. "Gee, I'm sixty-seven. I've got this disease of old age. I'll start slowing down because society tells me I'm supposed to slow down, because that's what a sixty-seven-year-old is supposed to do, so I guess I will." This is what we call a self-fulfilling prophecy. It happens just because you believe it. We really do live in our own realities and our own realities are derived from our own thinking more than anything. Changing our thinking is what we are striving for — changing the realities we hold between our ears.

Ageism

Earlier in this book mention was made of a thing called "ageism." This is a very destructive prejudice which generates behavior which discriminates against older people simply because they are old. It is made up of myths and stereotypes that are, at best, half-truths and unfounded assumptions. We have become very sensitized in our culture to other prejudices, to other "isms." Racism and sexism are two prime examples. Very few people would not react negatively now if someone came up and said, "Well, you know this race is more intelligent than the other race." We would all recognize this as a racist statement. Or if someone came up and said, "Women's place is in the home and that's where they need to stay." This is clearly a sexist statement. But we are just beginning to get sensitized to ageism. "Don't worry about it, he's kind of old. We can't do much for him. Just let him sit there, it's all right. He's seventy-three, you know." Such ageist statements are as ravaging to the person as a racist statement or a sexist statement would be. We as a society still subscribe to much of what ageism preaches. In itself, the very fact that our society is getting older will help solve a lot of these problems. Meanwhile we have this notion in our society which some sociologists have referred to as the YAVIS syndrome. The YAVIS syndrome states that all of us would rather deal with people who are young, attractive, verbal, intelligent, and successful. Anybody else somehow is not quite up to standard. Growing older certainly doesn't measure up. To what degree is the YAVIS syndrome within us? We have to examine ourselves.

Specific Problems of Adult Children Caregivers

The first part of this chapter was designed as a general backdrop against which you can project this second section which deals with the specific problems and challenges that you have as caregiver to your own parents. Not only do you have to deal with the various *general* myths and stereotypes but you also have another whole set that is uniquely your own. You are your parents' child. You were brought up in a specific setting and you have established a relationship with your parents that is uniquely your own. The way that you consciously or subconsciously perceive how your parents cared for you when you were young has a tremendous impact on your ability to care for your parents now. They were your primary sources or resources for you to learn how to deal with the outside world.

Your father was the primary person from whom you learned how to deal with the males in your life. Your mother was the person who taught you how to deal with the females, regardless of your own gender. Furthermore, in their interaction between themselves, your parents taught you how to relate, to them and to all others. This learning has become part of your very being. That's why you need to get "in touch" with your past. You need to understand how you feel about the way you grew up and what you want or need now from your parents. Some of this is hard to deal with because it is very deep and psychological. If your home was a battleground, if you remember your home as being filled with bickering and fighting and criticism, then in what position will you find yourself dealing with your aging parents now? What assumptions are you making about your parents? There will always be some assumptions and viewpoints from your childhood, some ideas and attitudes from the past which are still influencing you. You need to identify and clarify them. If these deep, controlling feelings remain unnoticed, you may be heading for trouble, not only for yourself but also for your aging loved one because your parent does not need a resentful, anxious, or depressed adult child coming at him or her with strong underlying feelings of anger and resentment about to surface.

Georgia's Story

Let's look at Georgia's story. Georgia was the second of seven children. She and her older sister were called upon very early to shoulder a large portion of the care for their younger brothers and sisters. This was especially so after her mother became ill. Her father was a rather active entrepreneur who enjoyed traveling, business dealings, and fraternizing with his friends down on the corner. His responsibility to the family generally ended with bringing home his paycheck. Georgia's interaction with her father centered around getting household chores done and child-care responsibilities. Consequently, Georgia got married at the age of nineteen. She eagerly got out of her home and began a family of her own. Now at age forty-four, Georgia's relationship with her father is very complicated. On the one hand she desires her father's recognition, his attention, and his love, something she feels she never got while growing up. On the other hand, she feels slighted and deprived by her father and harbors deep personal resentments and anger about all of this deprivation. Consequently, Georgia is almost emotionally paralyzed when interacting with her father. She wants a relationship and yet somehow wants to even the balance for the inconsistencies and the injustices she feels were a result of her father's domineering and critical attitude during her childhood.

Fortunately, Georgia found a counselor who could help her sort through these family issues so she didn't allow her negative feelings to intensify. She was able to recognize the heretofore unconscious revenge she harbored against her father and was able to dispose of it through learning what and how to forgive. In this way she formed the vehicle to honor her father and heal herself.

Saying No

Why do so many adult children have such a difficult time saying "no" to their aging parent? Somehow there is a feeling that if they did so they would pay a horrible price for it. This person has given so much to them, therefore they owe this much or more in return. What could be that horrible price? One of the prices could be the withdrawal of parental love. When you were a small child, perhaps two or three years old, your parents were like demi-gods to you. Their word was law. They were like two giants towering above you. Their love for you provided the emotional sustenance you needed to nurture you. Even though you were very young, you implicitly knew you needed their love. When you felt their love, you felt secure and safe. On those occasions when you were disciplined and they temporarily appeared to withdraw their love from you, your world became hostile and fearsome. If you lost the love of your parents, you would suffer an emotional death. This sense of impending doom, this insecurity in the form of anxiety you felt way back when you were very young, can still be felt today. If you lose your parents' love, your unconscious mind fears that you just might suffer an emotional death. "If you don't eat your dinner, you are going to be sent to bed." What that amounted to was "I'm not going to love you if you don't do the things I want you to do." That record or tape was recorded time and again in your head. What do you think is playing back to the adult child now in the relationship with the parent?

Guilt

The fear of withdrawal of love can generate other feelings such as rejection and punishment, as well as an overriding guilt. "I feel so guilty when I say no. How can I say no?" I have people that come and see me about dealings with their older parent who are convinced that they can't break out. I believe that they can, but they won't because they are unwilling to face the tremendous weight of guilt their conscience would burden them with if they said "no." What is driving them? What motivates them to do that or to be so incapacitated? At the very base of this insecurity is a psychological fear, a fear which paralyzes. They fear they are not living up to expectations. Has this happened to you? Even if these expectations become rather distorted and overburdening when your parents get older, you still want to satisfy them because you want their love and approval.

Reaction Formation

Sometimes the reason you can't say no is because you are secretly angry and use reaction formation as a defense. Suppose you are secretly angry, but that anger is too scary for you to bring up to a conscious level. You have said to yourself: "You shouldn't be angry at your mother." Of course you shouldn't be angry at your mother, but you are! So you go through an unconscious psychological process called reaction formation. You are not even aware you are doing it. It allows you to think "I'm not angry with you. I love you." This can happen with you and your aging parent because of some of the uncertainties and insecurities you feel due to all the discipline, the structure, and perhaps the sense of "unfairness" you felt as a child. "Make sure you get an A. Got to get A's in school. I want you to lead the class. I want you to play tennis like a pro. You've got to play football." All these demands and expectations make up so much of what our relationship was with our parents. Way down deep we may resent them. Different parents give them in different measures.

What Can Be Done?

Here are six ideas to help you avoid the obstacles that prevent you from having a quality relationship with your aging parent.

1. Get as much knowledge about aging as you possibly can. In this case, knowledge is power. When you have an understanding of the aging process you will have power to change things.

2. You need to clarify your relationship with your parents now, as it exists, and compare it to what formerly existed when you were young. How do you recall your parents' behavior? Do you recall them being caring and loving? Or were they critical, judgmental, domineering, and authoritarian? Was it somewhere in-between? Most relationships with parents are somewhere in the middle. Parents aren't perfect. Many children feel that their parents are really treading on them. To some degree that still may be working against you.

3. You need to determine how much you can give. How much can you give without putting an undue strain on your own relationship with your mate or with your kids or with your God? Where do

you draw the line? There is no simple answer. I can't tell you where. This is a personal and familial judgment, and the only way you can make a good judgment on this is to have knowledge about the aging process to clarify where you are with your relationship with your own parents.

4. When you recognize that your parents need something or some service and you are unable, for whatever reasons, to provide it for them, find substitutes. We are living in an increasing service-oriented society and there are many people who can help you: home help care agencies, Meals on Wheels, friendly care-giver visitors, and many church programs. Don't feel guilty about getting substitutes because they may be able to do it better than you. Your parent doesn't have to play parent to them as he or she does with you.

5. Become clear and direct in your communication with your parents. You will learn much more about this in the chapter which deals with communication. The interaction most adult children have with their parents is not clear and direct. There are many subtleties present and that leaves a very wide range for mis-interpretation, both on the part of the aging parent and on the part of the adult child. "What did she really mean by that?"

6. Take a step back. Recognize that you are not the "happiness provider" for your aging parents. They are living their own lives. Maybe the way they are living their lives is not the way you would want them to do it, nor is it the way you would want to live your own life, but it is the way they are living theirs. Nowhere is it written in the Bible that you have an obligation to change their lifestyle. Honoring your aging parent has much more to do with accepting and supporting them than it does with trying to change them. We have this idea that "Well, I'm her daughter (or son), so I can really communicate with her." This is a fallacy. Someone who is much more objective can probably communicate better than you can. That's why there are professional people like psychologists and counselors and clergy. Use the helpers that are available to you.

Personal Sharing Sheet

1. Identify some personal attitudes about older persons that may hinder your relationship.
2. What (if any) myths did you believe about older persons?
3. To what degree are you prejudiced against older persons — an ageist?
4. What personality characteristics do you remember about your parents from childhood that could act as a special barrier for you today in dealing effectively with your aging parent?
5. To what degree should you (can you) shoulder the care-giving relationship for your parent(s)?

5

How to Communicate With Your Aging Parents

The first chapter pointed out that we have to move away from the childhood notion of simple obedience toward the creation of an adult-level quality, caring relationship.

An essential element of such a relationship has to be good communication. Communication is at the heart of any genuine relationship. In your relationship with your aging loved one you are not there to handle finances, although handling finances may be part of the problem. You are not there to vacuum the living room rug, although periodically that may be part of it as well. You are not there to provide all the happiness for your aging parent. No, you are there to honor your aging parent and that means to enjoy a quality relationship with him or her. Our goal, at this point, is to look at the notion of communication, the beating heart of a quality relationship.

Active Listening

Active listening establishes trust. Many times a certain lack of trust can develop between an adult child and an aging parent. This

can be carried to an extreme, producing high levels of suspiciousness and even paranoia. If this has happened in your
situation, you would no doubt welcome some good news. It's not
an exaggeration to state that this lack of trust can be practically
eliminated by learning and becoming adept at "active listening."
Nor is that the only good thing that will happen. Self-esteem
improves once you allow a person to self-disclose and to express
his or her feelings. So, by actively listening you are automatically
raising your aging parent's self-esteem. When we listed the basic
human needs of older persons in Chapter Two, one of the first was
raising self-esteem. Moreover, active listening gives you the opportunity to understand your parent more fully. How can you genuinely know him or her if you don't listen? Using this skill also gives
your parents a chance to clarify their ideas, their thoughts, and
their feelings.

Another need outlined in Chapter Two was the need to find
solutions to problems, i.e., to establish problem-solving patterns
that will help your parents make decisions on their own.

These are some of the things that active listening can do. What's
involved in this skill and how does a person acquire it? It is more
than merely not talking, although being silent at times is certainly
part of it. Sometimes that's the problem. Silence is difficult for
most of us.

Silence

A professor told this story about one of his students. He received
a call one afternoon from a young man who said, "I'd like to come
over and talk with you." The professor agreed. The student came
over and sat down in the professor's office. The first five minutes
went by and the student didn't say anything. The professor didn't
say anything either. Ten minutes went by. Fifteen minutes went by.
Thirty minutes went by and still nothing was said. Not one word
between the two individuals was exchanged. After a time the
student got up and left. Two weeks later the professor got a call
from the student saying, "I want to thank you so much for all you
did for me that afternoon. You really helped me a lot." Actually
that professor did help the student, he didn't feel the need to fill up

that afternoon with words the student obviously didn't need. Much, however, was communicated in that silence. He communicated respect, understanding, and concern. He was giving to that student exactly what was needed — time in front of a caring, understanding presence of an authority perhaps, or of a father figure, simply "to be." Perhaps this is what your aging parents need too. They need simply "to be."

Attending

If real communication is to occur, a certain intensity of presence is demanded. But this presence, this "being with" another person, is impossible without attending. Attending seems so simple a concept to grasp that you might wonder why it's mentioned here. As simple as attending is, it's amazing how often people fail to attend to one another.

Physical Attending

Your body plays a large part in your communication. You should adopt a posture of involvement in your interactions with your aging loved one. The basic elements of physical attending can be recalled through the help of the acronym SOLER:

S - face the person *squarely*. This posture says "I'm available to you."

O - adopt an *open* posture. Crossed arms and legs are at least minimal signs of lessened involvement.

L - *lean* toward the other. This is another sign of availability or presence.

E - maintain good *eye* contact. Look directly at the person you are speaking with.

R - be relatively *relaxed*. This says "I'm at home with you."

This lineup is not meant to be followed in any rigid way. Attending should serve the communication process; it is not an end in itself. The important thing to learn is that your body *does* communicate — for good or ill.

Psychological Attending

If you are constantly delivering messages with your body, the same is true for your aging parent. He or she is also sending many bodily messages of which you should be aware. When you are tuned in to these messages, you are using psychological attending. This means you are alert to both nonverbal behavior (such as gestures and facial expressions) and what is called paralinguistic behavior (such as tone of voice, inflection, spacing of words, emphasis, and pauses). It has been shown that the nonverbal and paralinguistic cues can contradict the surface meaning of the words. For example, tone of voice can indicate that a verbal "no" is really a "yes."

One of the ways to become an active listener is to use what are called subtle encouragements to talk. These subtle encouragements can take many forms. Small responses such as "um-hum," "I understand," nods of the head, and repeating the last words that your aging parents just said to you are all excellent examples of encouragement to talk. Your mom may say, "Gee, I think I would like to go shopping." A good response might be simply to say, "Go shopping?" It sounds awkward when explained, but when it is actually done in the real world it becomes not at all unnatural. This says to your parent, "I'd like to hear more about this." I think many times we cut people short. There might be a lot more that they want to say.

Judging and Criticizing

Another important skill you can put to good use in dealing with your aging parent is nonjudgmental behavior. It appears that we have a lot of *shoulds* and *oughts* in us. A well-known psychologist, Albert Ellis, maintains that all this "shoulding" is very abusive. Sometimes it's very subtle like, "You know, Mother, I think you ought to get more exercise." Your mother may need more exercise; her doctor has probably told her to get more exercise. But there is an implicit judgment or criticism in that statement. How will it most likely be received? With resistance! People usually respond with resistance whenever unsolicited advice or criticism is given. Human beings are ornery. They almost always do exactly the opposite of what you'd like them to do.

Nonjudgmental behavior means learning to suspend your own evaluation in deference to your parents' opinion. They may be wrong and you may know that they are wrong. As long as this mistake is not health-threatening, your job is to let it go. If your mother is seventy-five years old and she hasn't exercised for sixty-five years, what makes you think she's going to start now? Judgmental behavior only drives you and your aging parent apart, not together.

Betty and Mrs. D

What follows is a dialogue which we will use as a case study. It is a conversation between Mrs. D and her daughter Betty. Betty says, "Hi, Mom. How are you doing today?" "Oh, not too good today," responds her mother. "What's wrong?" asks Betty. "I'm just so dragged out; I can't seem to get going," sighs her mother. Betty says, "Well, you shouldn't spend so much time watching TV. If you got a little exercise like the doctor suggested you wouldn't feel so tired all the time." Mrs. D responds, "Oh, what does he know." Betty says, "Well, anybody could see you need to get up and get around. You don't go down to the senior citizen's center like I want you to. You refuse to invite people in for fear they will criticize you. You're just sitting here slowly dying. How do you think that makes me feel?" Mrs. D says, "I just wish I could be around when you get older."

Betty says, "Oh, you are just depressed because nobody calls you anymore." Mrs. D says, "They do so call, they just can't come over." Betty says, "Mom, you know that's not true. You just won't look at reality anymore. What's the matter with you? Are you taking all the medication your doctor prescribed? I'll just bet you aren't." Mrs. D, holding back tears, says, "Betty, why are you so hard on me?" Betty says, "I'm not being hard, you just think I am because you're not doing what you know is right." Mrs. D, who is now crying, says, "I try, Betty, I try." Betty, now moved with guilt, says, "Now, now, Mother, it's all right. You are going to be just fine." Mrs. D says, "Do you think so, Betty?" Betty says, "I'm sure of it, just do what the doctor and I tell you. If you'll do that you'll be fine." End of conversation.

What Went Wrong?

Why did this conversation degenerate into a verbal battle and then into an exercise of seeing who could lay the most guilt on the other? What went wrong? For one thing, Betty gave unsolicited advice. As was mentioned, most people don't want advice and that seems to be especially true of older people. If you do that with your aging parents, you will find that they have probably thought of all the things you're suggesting anyway. Their problem is uniquely theirs and the solution you devise will be uniquely yours and probably nonfunctional for them. One of Betty's statements was, "You shouldn't spend so much time watching TV." Notice the *should* statement in there. Even if these words were said in a benign and caring way, they still have all sorts of negative overtones. First, they imply incapability. Secondly, it sets up an authoritarian relationship. Without realizing it, Betty was asserting "I'm the boss and you are the child." Thirdly, if Mrs. D really wanted advice, she'd ask for it. Fourthly, advice is always given from your own point of view and usually doesn't take your aging parent's perspective into consideration.

What else did Betty do wrong? She analyzed and interpreted Mrs. D's words with statements like, "You're just sitting around here slowly dying" or "Oh, you are just depressed because no one calls you anymore." Such analyses are inherently disrespectful, even when they are not meant to be. Next, Betty's statement, "You just won't look at reality anymore," was critical and unnecessary. Another remark by Betty, "You're not doing what you know is right," is also off the mark. Isn't Betty really saying "You're not doing what *I* think is right"? Besides, most amateur analyses and interpretations are incorrect. And research has shown that interpretations rarely, if ever, change behaviors. No wonder Betty's approach didn't work.

False Reassurance

The next thing that Betty did was to offer her mother false reassurance. There is a place for reassurance. It is when you know beyond a doubt that the situation is going to turn out the way you portray it. But to say things like, "Don't worry, everything is going to be all right" or "This will all pass and you'll be your old self again soon" is damaging because it's only a temporary fix. Betty didn't really know what was going to happen. Improvement of her mother's health may or may not be in the future. Even though a younger person may believe that things will get better because they always seem to, the same idea does not necessarily apply to an older person. With the elderly it's more likely that the situation will not improve. We might want to deny this fact. I've heard family members talk to people who they know are terminally ill and be so fearful of the impending death that they completely deny it. The nephew comes in, "Don't worry, Uncle Fred, next week you're going to be out fishing again." Since it's much more probable that Uncle Fred is going to die soon, it is not at all reassuring to tell him he's going to be fishing next week. Uncle Fred needs to confront his death, not deny it.

Betty reacted strongly to her mother's statement: "I'm not feeling too well." What rose up in her was anger. She wasn't clear why she felt that way. One thing that it meant was that she was reacting to her mother rather than responding to her. She reacted instead of thinking, "OK, I'm feeling some anger here, but I'm not going to let this anger interfere with how I should act." She first expressed this anger at her mother and then, as soon as her mother began to cry, what did she do? She felt guilty. Acting out of guilt is another way to dishonor your aging parent. Betty allowed this feeling of guilt to take over. It made her falsely reassure her mother. This scenario has probably repeated itself many times. False reassurance engenders dependence. What Betty is basically saying is "You can't think for yourself, so I'll think for you."

Betty is really a very nice person. Unfortunately, she fell into many traps that were part of the situation. With everybody else, Betty is just wonderful. It's only with her mother that she has a problem. What would have been a better approach?

Exploration

The first skill she could have exercised is "active listening." There is another related skill which also would have served Betty well. It's a process known as exploration. Exploration means to identify the facts that can bring meaning to a confused person or situation. How is it done? You as a caregiver need to develop these three skills: the ability to (1) clarify issues, (2) recognize problems, and (3) establish life goals.

Beyond active listening and using exploration, Betty could also have helped matters a great deal if she had searched for the *exact* meaning of her mother's words. For example, when Mrs. D said that she didn't feel "too good today," what was she really trying to say? Was it "I'm really not doing well at all"? If this was her meaning, was she referring to not feeling well emotionally or not feeling well physically? There is a great deal of vagueness in her statement. This is where the skill of "making concrete" is very important.

Concretize

One of my jobs in the hospital where I work is to teach physicians. As young interns they learn how important it is to search out any facts that may have a bearing upon their patient's condition. For instance, suppose you came to your physician and said, "Doctor, yesterday I didn't feel very well." If your doctor did nothing but handed you a piece of paper and said, "Here's a prescription. I want you to take these three times a day," what would you think? Since he didn't find out any of the details of the sickness — if it had an onset two weeks ago or only yesterday, whether the condition was acute or chronic — how could he diagnose it properly and suggest the correct treatment? His mistake was that he was not *concrete*. He didn't make it specific enough.

Now let's apply this to your conversation with your elderly parents. In trying to discover the meaning of a statement, you must continually strive for "concreteness." If you don't concretize things that they say to you, how can you be helpful? In Betty's case, what is the true meaning behind her mother's statement about not feeling well? Was her meaning, ''I don't know what to do to help myself''? Was it that she was confused? How many different interpretations could there be of Mrs. D's statement? Or when Mrs. D said, ''Oh, what does he know,'' referring to her doctor, was she expressing difficulty in following his instructions? Or was this an expression of anger at her physician and maybe at herself? You can never be absolutely sure of what your aging parent is trying to say. That is why the effort to make things as concrete and as exact as possible is so important.

Accurate Empathy

Another skill of good communication is called ''accurate empathy.'' Basically, this means expressing that you understand what others are saying or feeling. You are walking in their shoes, so to speak. You need to communicate empathy to your parents so any conversations you have with them don't begin to resemble Betty and Mrs. D's war zone. Accurate empathy isn't too difficult to do. It takes some practice and some alertness. It means that you restate what your parents said. You can tack in front of your restatement a phrase like, ''You mean'' or ''Mom, I didn't quite understand what you meant when you said . . . '' or ''Could you help me out? What are you really saying here?'' It's what I call peeling the artichoke of feelings until you finally discover its heart.

This may sound very simple but it could have a profound effect on your relationship. Of course, it has to be done on a consistent basis. The positive results will not materialize overnight. However, in time you will notice a real difference. It may be confusing to your aging parent at first, so you may want to introduce it gradually; but over time its benefits will become obvious to all.

Like a Mirror

This next skill is a variant of the skill of empathy and is called ''reflection of feelings'' or ''response to feelings.'' Table one is a list of feeling words arranged in a very special way. Across the top are seven basic feelings. These are: happy, sad, warm, angry, cold, confused, and weak. You will notice that there are three levels of

FEELINGS LIST

LEVELS OF INTENSITY	HAPPY	SAD	WARM	ANGRY	COLD	CONFUSED	WEAK
STRONG	ecstatic overjoyed joyous	dismal sorrowful gloomy	passionate fervent enthusiastic	infuriated incensed enraged	impudent vulgar abusive	bewildered trapped perplexed	shattered powerless exhausted
MILD	gay great up	melancholy dejected downcast	affectionate close cordial	disgusted irritated inflamed	discourteous impolite fresh	flustered muddled mixed-up	impotent frail withered
WEAK	glad fortunate contented	cheerless somber unhappy	sunny alive responsive	mad frustrated sore	ungracious sassy cool	unsure embarrassed uncomfortable	decayed spent broken down

intensity: strong, mild, and weak. None of these words is foreign to you. They are the most powerful words you can say to your aging parent. I implore you to sprinkle your conversations with them because they will give you power (in the good sense of that word) and they will also empower your loved ones.

How do you use them? Let's take a look. Feelings are the movers of the drama of life. Everything you do is motivated by a feeling. The driving force behind feelings is your thoughts. Feelings drive your behavior. If you can clarify feelings, you are necessarily clarifying your thoughts. Many of us have not learned how to express our feelings. But feelings are a measure of the warmth, emotional responsiveness, and attentiveness in a relationship. Unfortunately, many of us have not had a good education in feelings. Fortunately, we can learn.

When you are talking with your parent, try to become like a mirror. Hold that mirror up to what your parent is saying. Let it reflect back the thoughts, the attitudes, and, most important, the feelings expressed by your aging parent. Every one of his or her words is weighted with feeling. The person who's best at picking out those feelings and reflecting them back is the person who can build the most quality into the adult-child/aging-parent relationship. This is a simple yet profound statement; a statement which can pay marvelous dividends in enriching your relationship. The positive results that you will be able to achieve with the skill of reflection of feelings will amaze you.

Examples

Let's look at some examples. An eighty-one-year-old woman lives in an extended-care facility. She says, ''One day just seems to mesh into another. They don't seem to be separate or distinct like they used to be.'' Perhaps your parents have said something like that. How do you respond? Do you say, ''You shouldn't think that way. Look at the sun, it's shining; before you know it the robins are going to be here and the crocuses are going to be up, and it's really a nice day, don't you think?''

Another way to respond would be: ''Mom, it sounds to me like you're feeling kind of gloomy today because your days seem to mesh into one another." Why is that a better response? For two reasons. One, you have identified a feeling and you've reflected it back; you have used the mirror of your mind. Two, you also have reflected back some of the content that she said to you. You may think that this is a simplistic, even depressing, way to respond to your mother. I can assure you, however, that a response like this will enrich the very heart of your relationship. It can also protect you from getting caught in the web of guilt, the feeling that it's somehow your fault that your mother is feeling so badly. Ultimately, responses such as these can prevent you from creating a dependent relationship.

Remember, you don't have to find solutions, you don't have to give advice, you don't have to express "Why don't you do this?" or "You shouldn't feel that way because. . . . " Forget all of that controlling behavior. Your aging parent is in the last days of his or her life. You don't want to think that after your parent leaves this planet, after he or she dies, that you have to ask yourself, "Did I handle this right, did I do this right?" If you are trying to "be with" your loved one in mind and heart, you're doing the right thing.

A seventy-seven-year-old man says, "I don't want to go to the hospital — those doctors don't know what they are doing. I'll never come out of there." You know that he's got an abdominal aneurysm, that he needs surgery, and if he doesn't get it he will die. Your helpful and caring response could be something like: "You feel enraged that you have to go into the hospital. You're also very worried about the outcome of the surgery the doctors have recommended." You don't say, "I'm sure those doctors know what they're doing," or "Well, don't worry about it because, you know, my uncle went in for the same exact operation you need. He's fine today. He's doing great." Maybe you want to get to that later, but what has to be done first? This man needs to get his anger out. He needs to express his worries. Let him do it. Let him get these emotions out in the open. That's what he needs. That's how you can be most helpful to him at this point. Eventually, as the conversation progresses, you might get to your uncle who had his abdominal aneurysm repaired with great results. But to get to that before you get to this man's feelings would be doing him a disservice and would be robbing you of a potential quality relationship with him.

Another example is an eighty-year-old woman who is in the hospital. She says, "Why do you keep asking me what day it is? Of course, I know what day it is. Stop doing that." So what do you say to this totally unnerved person? You could say, "Sounds to me like you are feeling very irritated because I keep asking you what day it is." With this response you've done two things. First, you've identified a feeling. Doing this is as emotionally comforting to an individual as hearing their own name spoken softly. Secondly, you have provided an understandable reason for having the feeling. In short, you have affirmed this woman, you have given her a holy gift, you have honored her.

Another example is a seventy-three-year-old man living in an extended-care facility who says, "You know, that head nurse has ice water in her veins. She never cracks a smile and she troops around here like a top sergeant." You could respond, "It sounds like you are feeling rather uncared for and rather unimportant here because the head nurse seems to be cold and uncaring toward you." What do you think this man's response will be back to you? He'll probably say, "Yea, you're right, that's exactly what I'm talking about and I wish she wouldn't do that." And you could then respond to him, "You wish she wouldn't do that?" "You're right," he might respond. "How did you know that I felt that way? How did you know?" You have just granted him the gift of emotional life and affirmation. You have honored him.

Conclusion

You have a choice when you communicate with your aging parent. You can focus primarily on the content of what is being said, or you can expand your focus to include the feelings behind the statements. If you focus on content alone you will find your relationship somehow lacking, shallow, and relatively unfulfilling. By focusing on feelings, however, you give life to your interactions, zest to your conversations, and most importantly of all, you add quality to your relationships and honor to your aging parent and yourself.

This chapter outlined a simple, sequential procedure you can follow to enhance your communication with your aging parent. That sequence is: (1) Exercise active listening. Demonstrate your interest in what is being said. (2) Be open to what is said. Do not judge, evaluate, or analyze; remain nonjudgmental. (3) Make sure you know what your aging parent is saying. Try to understand the real meaning of the communication; help your aging parent to be as concrete as possible. (4) Identify the feeling or feelings which are motivating your aging parent to make this statement. (5) Recognize and communicate back an affirming reason why your aging parent feels the way he or she does.

This five-step procedure can be summarized as follows. Suggested "response leads" are included.

1. Active listening

2. Attending posture

3. Clarify meaning; be concrete
   a. "You mean . . . "
   b. "I hear you saying . . . "
   c. "Could I check this out . . . "
   d. "Help me understand. You're saying . . . "

4. Identify the motivating feelings
   a. "You feel . . . "
   b. "So you're feeling . . . "
   c. "It must be difficult for you to feel so . . . "
   d. "How do you feel about that?"

5. Give an affirming and understanding reason for the feeling
   a. You feel _____
      because _____
   b. I wonder if you're feeling _____
      because _____
   c. Could it be you feel _____
      because _____
   d. Your feeling of _____
      is understandable to me since _____

Personal Sharing Sheet

Now you have an outline and description of good communication. This can help you honor your aging parent. Successful communication leads to a maximum level of honor! Practice your new skills on the following cases:

1. Seventy-one-year-old widower father says to oldest son: "Your brother hasn't called me for a month."
2. Seventy-four-year-old mother calling from her apartment: "You better not come to get me today for dinner. I'm just feeling too low to come over." (Said to you the morning of the family celebration which has been planned for some time.)
3. Eighty-year-old mother calling from resident care facility: "There is no one to talk to around here; no one cares; I want to go home!"
4. Seventy-eight-year-old mother, living at home with husband: "Your father is getting so irritable. Either he sits in front of the TV or he gets angry at me."
5. Eighty-three-year-old mother, three years after death of spouse: "I'm so tired. I just want to die."

6

Helping Your Older Parents Develop More Positive and Meaningful Attitudes

Several years ago an important book appeared: *Passages,* by Gail Sheehy. Basically stated, Sheehy's ideas are that we continue to grow our entire life, that we are constantly going through cycles of what she calls transitions and stages. Transitions last between one and three years. They are potentially chaotic periods between the end of one stage and the beginning of another. If there is a weak link in your life-chain, it is the transition link. That is where it is most likely to break. If you are prone to depression, for example, it may appear first during a transition. The same would be the case for the onset of migraine headaches, ulcers, or whatever. The evidence suggests that all of this usually develops or worsens during the stressful time of a transition. So, transitions are those times in your life which can be potentially traumatic, tempestuous, and extremely disconcerting. You are being pushed to make an important change.

Stages

Transitions link together those phases in your life called stages. Stages are typically seven to eight years in length (but these chronological demarcation points are different in each person). In contrast to transitions, your life during stages is basically placid. You are dealing with the same developmental tasks over and over. Your life is smooth, there is little change occurring, no crises to speak of, no bumps in the road, no critical junctures where you must decide which way you should go. Life during a stage sails along pretty well.

Transitions

But back to the transitions. To name a few, there is adolescence, then the launching phase where a person moves out of his home of origin. These are followed perhaps by "coupling" when you develop an intimate relationship with a special person. Then comes the so-called "age 30 transition" when you deepen your resolve and develop commitments in your life. Now comes the infamous mid-life transition with all of its turmoil and decision making. The family launching transition is next when the children leave the home, followed by a time of reorganization called the "empty nest" transition. Pre-retirement is next; quickly on its heels comes the retirement event and the hopeful development of a new life-style.

It's important to think of transitions as challenges. Instead of backing into a transition with your eyes closed, welcome it as a time of challenge, an opportunity for growth, and a time when you can change for the better. Researchers studying stress have found that the most potent stress reducer is your own attitude. Those persons who can conceive of stress as a challenge, as a time of commitment, and as a chance to grow and change instead of withdrawing from it, are those persons who are the most emotionally healthy.

When we apply this notion of transition and stage to older persons, we come up with some very interesting points. Some experts believe that the last decades of one's life are best defined as one long transition (rather than as a stage) because the older person is called upon to make so many changes during this period. This contradicts a commonly accepted myth that it is a time of serenity and calm where the old couple sit on the front porch in their rocking chairs and nothing much happens. Actually, a tremendous amount of change is taking place at this time. Think of the adjustments that older people are asked to make in their lives. Think of the coping mechanisms that have to be called upon. And all this is happening at a time in their life when their resources are dwindling rather than growing.

Six Life Arenas

These notions of life transitions and life stages can be further developed when we consider the six life arenas. Not only do you have changes occurring in your life as a whole but now, by introducing the idea of arenas, it is possible to conceive of these many changes occurring all at the same time. Have you ever been to a three-ring circus? Under the big top there are three rings or arenas where different things are happening in each one all at the same time. The lion tamer is in one arena, the clowns are in the second, and in the third you find the acrobats or the lady on the horse. The spotlight is moving from one ring or arena to another. First it's on the clown; then it's on the lion tamer, and then it's on the lady on the horse. Your focus of attention changes from one arena to another even though action continues in each. Your life is not a three-ring circus; it is a six-ring circus. You have six rings or arenas in your life and different things are happening in each of them. Sometimes you focus on one, sometimes on another. You can think of each arena in terms of roles, distinguishing characteristics, how much energy and time is invested in each, etc. Let me try to define these arenas for you. Incidentally, they are not listed in any order of priority; each arena is important.

Career Arena

The first one is called the career arena. It is defined as everything that you think, feel, and do in the world of work. Included is everything that is related to your job or career, i.e., your education and specialized training, the route you drive to your job, the people you work with, resting from work when you come home in the evening, and so on. These are all things that could be looked upon as being in the career arena. What kind of roles are there in this arena? Laborer, professional person, wage earner, homemaker, etc. In our society, work is looked on as a central task in our lives. From your earliest days you are given clear messages to go out there and get a job so that you can support yourself and your family. So you pour a lot of your life energy into this arena called career. As a matter of fact, sometimes people put so much energy into their career that they forget that they have five other arenas.

Family Arena

Number two is family. What kind of roles do you play in the family arena? Mother, father, sister, brother, aunt, uncle, daughter, son, grandmother, grandfather — these are all roles you could be playing. Another extremely important role that is played out in the family is that of learner. We learn more from our families than we learn anyplace else in our whole world, our whole lives. These lessons in our families are going to be with us for a long time. You do, however, have the ability to modify any of these; to determine whether or not you want this particular learning or some other. You can change it if you want to.

Intimacy Arena

The life arena of intimacy is number three. This includes all your relationships with other people. This runs the gambit from the bank teller with whom you have a relationship because he or she knows your bank book, account amount, etc., to your family and friends with whom you share deeper, more intimate parts of your relationships. You share a bit of yourself with the bank teller and intimacy at its most basic level is sharing. In fact, you might share a part of yourself with the teenagers who work at the fast food restaurant; they may know your preferences, whether it's a burger or a fish fillet sandwich. Beyond service providers you have your workmates, your acquaintances all the way up through your friends.

We move now to the person or persons with whom you are the most intimate. Intimacy again is defined as the amount, level, and quality of sharing that you have with another person. The more you share of yourself, the more you share your innermost thoughts, your innermost feelings, your deeply personal reactions to the world, the more intimate you are. We all need intimates, confidantes, people to whom we can talk. Many mental health research studies have shown that those people who are the most emotionally healthy have at least one other person with whom they can share their innermost thoughts; with whom they can be intimate. Intimacy is a health-producing item in your life; and so it is with older persons as well.

Inner Life Arena

Arena number four is your inner life. As the intimacy arena contained your relationship with other people, so your inner life is your relationship with yourself. What's in the inner life arena? All of your self-concepts are in there. Notice I said self-concepts; plural, not self-concept. We do not have just one idea about ourselves. We have many self-concepts, we wear many different hats in all the six life arenas. In the intimacy arena we have self-concepts of ourselves as a friend. Am I a good friend? Am I loyal? From the family life arena: Am I a good provider? a good homemaker? From the inner life arena itself: Am I an honest person? trustworthy? We've got a whole range of self-concepts that we project all the time. All of this is gathered together in our inner life — what we think of ourselves; how well we regard ourselves. There is also a dark side to this. The emotion of guilt that can so burden adult children is in this inner life arena. In some people it seems to have taken over completely. Guilt interferes with your positive feelings about yourself more than any other emotion.

Another aspect of your inner life is your relationship with your body. Perhaps sometimes you think of your body as your entire self, the real you. But deep down you know that your body is only part of you, an extremely important part, but not your total self. You acknowledge that you also have a spiritual soul, that you are a body-soul unit, a material-spiritual being who is one person.

This mysterious body-soul relationship makes itself known in many ways throughout your life, in your striving for beauty and goodness, in your longing for love, in your thirst for justice in an imperfect world, and in other ways that could be described as "noble."

Looking at it from a somewhat different angle, there's also a time when you become especially conscious of your body. It is when sickness enters the picture. You realize how vulnerable you are. It's like your body has betrayed you. Probably most people take their health and their body for granted, and when it fails them they are genuinely surprised. How do older people react when this happens? They start realizing that the end they knew was coming is definitely on its way. They realize they are mortal. This is not meant in a morbid sense. Dying is part of living. Dying is as natural as being born.

Leisure Arena

Number five is the leisure arena. Leisure is defined as that which we do when we don't have to do anything else. The whole idea of fun and play is contained here. Yet for many people this leisure arena is the most discounted of any in their lives. Americans have a very strong work ethic. There is nothing wrong with that until it begins to overpower us and we pump so much energy into it that the other arenas become anemic. There are people who have time for everything but leisure. Yet leisure is the one arena that can be changed today. You can't easily change your career arena today. You can't change your intimacy arena today. The same goes for the family arena or inner life arena — to substantially change these would take a great deal of time and energy. The leisure arena, however, can be changed this afternoon. You can decide right now that you are going to go to the movies. You have changed your life. You said, "I'm going to have some fun. I'm going to go to a movie. I don't want that movie to have any kind of message. I just want to have fun."

It's a healthy sign that a new kind of counselor is arising in our culture today, the leisure counselor. These experts in R and R tell us that leisure is a central, life-giving arena rather than a secondary one. What goes on in this arena has two primary purposes: rest and relaxation for the body and enrichment for the mind. Each of these objectives is crucial for you to achieve balance . . . crucial for both you as the adult child and for your aging parent.

Spiritual Life Arena

Last and certainly not least, an arena in which your aging parent can gain great personal satisfaction is the spiritual life arena. This arena encompasses the relationship a person has with God. It's true that some research studies have found that religious participation does not increase with age, but that there is a slight decrease. However, these studies were too narrowly constructed. They measured only participation in religious activities, i.e., how often a person goes to church, as the sole criterion of religiousness (here a number of "external" factors such as health and transportation problems probably play large roles). Moreover, it's very difficult to measure a change in a person's internal relationship with God. My nonscientific survey of older persons tells me that, as the shadows lengthen, older people do try to develop a more intimate relationship with God. Adult children can foster this development by praying with their parents, speaking about spiritual issues and relationships, and generally raising the level of awareness of and participation in religious activities and events.

But your aging loved one need not be only on the receiving end of all this. Quite the contrary. Respected theologian Bernard Häring offers some insightful comments about this: "And now the Church is discovering that the senior citizens themselves can be an almost inexhaustible reservoir of Samaritans, wounded healers who, like the *elders* of the earliest Christian tradition, are willing and able to bring their life experience and generosity creatively into the life of the community. . . . Both the Church and society have to revise their ideas about the elderly. . . . We would find that persons of this age group not only can better recognize their own situation but also can help others to resolve their problems in a creative way and put their capacities to the service of those aging persons most in need. . . . A modern revival of the ancient institute of the 'elders' and 'widows' could bring new contributing forces to the whole pastoral and healing mission of the Church. And, in this, many people could find, in the last decades of their life, their highest fulfillment by becoming helpers of the Divine Healer.''

Life Review

Your aging parents perform roles in each of these six life arenas. You need to view your loved ones in these settings. Once you have done that, ask yourself: How can I help my aging parent toward a more positive and meaningful attitude? Here are a few things you can do.

One way to help is by conducting a *life review.* What does this mean? *Life review* is a specialized term originated by Dr. Robert Butler. In every transition in your life, whether it's turning twenty-one, deciding on a mate, having children, experiencing ''empty nest'' syndrome, living through retirement backlash, etc., you conduct a kind of ''life review'' within yourself without even realizing it. One of the hallmarks of a transition is that it's a time for looking back at your life and asking, ''How am I doing? Is this the way I want to be conducting my life? Are there ways I could change it?'' Normally, that's healthy. Unfortunately, some people look back at their life and start digging up all sorts of regrets. ''I should have done this. I should have done that. I wish I hadn't done so-and-so.'' Even though people know that such thinking is self-defeating, they still continue to engage in it. How does life review avoid this pitfall, this extremely negative approach? Let's take a closer look at it.

Life review is a process whereby your aging parent can review his or her life in a positive, orderly manner. This type of healthy reminiscing enables the person to search for and uncover some of the deeper meanings underlying specific past events. This frequently helps the individual resolve long-standing conflicts. This is why all people, especially older persons, like to talk about their life in earlier days. There is an instinctive desire to "tie up all the loose ends." Of course, talking about the past all of the time is unhealthy and may be a sign that a person needs professional help. But well-ordered reminiscing, when done in a positive, sharing way, has been shown to help people, especially older ones, to live a richer, fuller, and healthier life. It's clear that this is not the idle wanderings of a deteriorating mind that can only "live in the past." Rather, it is the carrying out of a vital and enriching task of the present.

All indications are that all older persons reminisce to a certain degree and that it is quite normal. They need to do this because their central life task in later years is to achieve integrity. They need to put their past life into a meaningful and purposeful whole. Life review helps them achieve this vital goal of wholeness and completeness. Besides generating purpose, structured reminiscence aids in the rediscovery of past strengths, capabilities, and interests; fosters feelings and expressions of love; enhances the realization that aging is a time of continued personal growth; facilitates interactions; fights depression and demoralization; combats social isolation; and stimulates memory.

A Priest and His Father

About three years ago a priest came to me for counseling. He was a very successful man who had been a priest for twenty years and was currently the pastor of a large parish. His mother had passed away but his father was still living. It was with this man that the problem lay. His father evidently had been a very critical person, at least that's the way this priest remembered him. Every time we would talk, I'd hear how his dad had been so involved in his work and how they had moved from place to place and how he never saw much of him and when he did there was always criticism, and on and on. Finally, I said, ''Don't you think it's time to resolve this? You know we keep going round and round this bush and we are not addressing your central issue.'' He said, ''What do you mean, resolve this issue? My childhood is my childhood, what can I do? It's over, I can't relive it.'' I said, ''No, you can't. But you can resolve it because this issue is having a tremendously negative impact upon your present life.'' It was preventing him from breaking out, from gaining freedom and direction, and from getting to his next developmental stage. It had him locked in a transition.

I said, ''You need to confront your father.'' ''Confront my father?'' he said. ''He's seventy-eight years old. It'll kill him.'' I said, ''Well, he's lived seventy-eight years now, he's probably a pretty sturdy old guy.'' ''No,'' he said, ''this would do him in. I'm a priest, you know. I'm supposed to exemplify kindness and compassion and understanding and all those other wonderful attributes.'' I said, ''You're hung up on your father. You are locked into a transition. You don't have any choice but to confront him.'' So then we worked on how he could confront him, how he could say: ''Look, Dad, I have some heavy ideas I've been carrying around since my childhood. I want to say these things to you because they're inside my heart and I need to vent them and I need you to listen. I don't need your condemnation or your criticism. I'm fifty years old. I'm trying to serve God. I think I'm doing what I'm supposed to be doing and yet I've got this hang-up with you inside of me. Help me!''

That was a day of great tumult in the priest's life. Everything was turned upside down. He confronted his own father. He resolved an issue. Do you know something? Not only did he walk away from that day with a whole new world view, but his father had also been carrying around great guilt inside himself all these years and this confrontation allowed him to get it all out — so much so that within two months the priest's father was freed and he remarried. This seventy-eight-year-old man had also been stuck in a transition that he couldn't break out of because of this push-pull antagonism that he felt from his son and the guilt that he was laying on himself. This resolution process brought the two of them together and sparks were flying all over the place. Those two men, father and son, walked away from that confrontation different people. They faced change; they took action on a life transition. Both of their lives got unstuck because of it.

Doing a Life Review

This is but one example of the power of the life review process. It can help people resolve deep-seated conflicts of the past and thereby start them building quality relationships here and now. How is this done in practice? How do you go about conducting a life review with your aging loved one?

Recall what was emphasized earlier. Remember how everyone's life experience can be viewed as being played out in six *arenas*. Recall also that people go through *transitions* and *stages* as they live their lives. And a characteristic of these transitions and stages is that they are filled with much *emotion and feeling*. You can help your aging parent put his or her life in proper perspective and make it understandable, clear, and meaningful *if* you can bring together these three elements — the life arenas, the transitions and stages, and the emotions experienced at those times — and focus them on your loved one's life story.

It took me several years but I finally noticed the obvious: People generally have a difficult time visiting older people, especially if they are in a nursing home and especially if they are adult children visiting their parents. They simply don't know what to say. "How's the food been, Mom? Been sleeping okay? How are your feet? Getting enough exercise?" To say the least, the quality of these visits leaves much to be desired. I was sure there was a better way. That's when the thought struck me: When you visit, why not spend a half hour going through a life review? Obviously you can't go through a whole life in half an hour, but you have a lot to talk about here. You've got six arenas. You've got about thirteen different transitions and several stages. You've got a whole horizon full of emotions that you can talk about. It doesn't have to be stiff and formal. "How did you feel, Mom, when you had your first child?" "How about dating?" "How many dates did you have?'' ''What did Granddad say to you when you first started dating?'' ''How about school? What was it like in those days? Remember some of your teachers' names in school?'' ''How did you feel at graduation?''

Your Parents' Emotional Life

Like most adult children, you may know very little about the *emotional* lives of your parents. You probably know most of the statistical things about them, the external ''facts.'' You know they got married in 1929; they had their first child in 1931; they lived through the Depression and it was tough times; they went through World War II and Dad was in the service. You know all that sort of stuff. But that's only an outer structure, sort of a facade of a person's life. That's not where people really *live*. Relationships are what give meaning to life. And the very heartbeats of all relationships are the emotions and feelings a person experiences as these life episodes are being lived.

Besides being very beneficial for your parents, your life review visits could also be very enriching for yourself. You needn't dread the next time you go see Mom. Rather, you can look forward to it because while you're learning a new chapter of her life you'll also be discovering your own emotional roots at the same time. In doing this, try to get as much of it down in writing as you can, or, even better, record it on tape. After all, your parents will not be with you someday. This is not said to stir up guilt feelings; it's simply a fact. It's also true that there will be people three or four generations down the road who would very much enjoy hearing what this person, your parent, was actually like.

Perhaps some of you have done this already with your parents in some small way. Each and every person in this world has a story to tell, and each story is well worth hearing. If this is true of everyone, even of the strangers who pass you on the street, how much more valuable would be your own parents' life story, a record of significant happenings in their life, all told in their own words. Do you see the potential here? Instead of looking on those visits to your parents as drudgery, instead of thinking, ''Oh my gosh, what am I going to say today?'' you can think about what you are going to do and what you will learn once you arrive. The first few life review visits might seem awkward with the note-taking or the tape recorder microphone out there . . . but after a while it will all seem very natural. Incidentally, one of the nice things about making a recording is that you can leave the tape with your mom for her to replay during the week if she wants to. Chances are, her listening will stir up other memories, ones she had almost forgotten, precious memories about her early life, about happy or sad moments, about her own parents or other relatives, or about you, her child, when you were very small.

Positive Effects

Once more, what are the positive effects of the life review process? First, it can help resolve conflict. There are times when everyone looks back and says: "Boy, I wish I'd done things differently then." It's at that point that you can look at your mom (or dad) and say, "You know, if I were in your shoes at that point in your life, I think I would have done the very same thing." "You would have?" will be the response. "I think I would have." Lo and behold, the conflict which had so tied up your parents begins to unravel. It's almost like receiving absolution. They are able to start thinking of themselves in more positive terms. They are more prepared to address the changes they need to make in their life now. They are being freed to create a greater peace, serenity, and wisdom in their hearts.

Let's say your mother begins to tell a story she has told many times before. What you should do is sit down with her and ask, "Mom, are you trying to tell me something? What is it here in this story that's so important? What changed in your life because of this story? Is this story somehow like what's going on now in your life?" If you can help your mother discover the underlying meaning of that story, why it is significant for her, you will be doing her a tremendous favor, you will be showing her the highest honor. You have the power and the ability to do that. You don't need a psychologist to do that . . . you can do that yourself. As a matter of fact, you are probably in a much better position to do that than a psychologist or anyone else.

Life review is a very realistic attempt to put one's entire life in proper perspective. Have you seen your aging parents depressed at one time or another? Have you seen them anxious? You know how hopeless you feel when they are like that. What can you do? Now your answer can be that you will try to develop a quality relationship with them through life review.

How to Begin

Of course, this has to be done gently. You can't go home tonight, or to the nursing home, or wherever your aging parent may be and say, "Guess what we are going to do right now? We are going to take out this legal pad and we're going to do a life review." You might start with looking through an old photo album together. Or you might ask about the family tree, or relatives you've lost track of, or where certain mementos came from. Stories are always important. There are so many questions to be asked. Think of all the changes that have occurred. Recall what was said in Chapter Five about effective communication. People open up when they realize they are really being listened to. Respect your aging parents by using the full range of skills of active listening. Attend to them fully, both physically and psychologically; become a mirror to their thoughts and emotions by reflecting back what was said, by being concrete, by seeking clarification of events, relationships, and feelings. Ask questions which begin with "what," "where," "how," or "when." Try not to ask "why" questions because that calls for a rational response to situations or feelings which many times do not have a logical explanation. As much as possible, get on the feelings level. Try to follow up responses with questions like: "How did you feel when that happened?" "What was it like to be in that position?" In addition to our "thought memory" we also have a "feelings memory," which is all the emotions associated with a particular event, etc. Sharing feelings brings people ever closer together.

"Generations ... the Game"

There is another tool available, a board game called "Generations . . . the Game." I developed this myself to assist families, especially adult children, conduct structured, orderly, and enriching life reviews. It also turned out to be fun. The object of the game is to respond to questions as clearly and completely as possible. This game was specially constructed to accomplish all the above mentioned goals regarding life review. I developed it because my efforts at training adult children to help their aging parents with life reviews were unsuccessful. Adult children understood the concept very well and were eager to begin but they simply couldn't seem to get started. The game can fill that need. Whenever you get stumped saying, "What questions should I ask now?" think of the six life arenas. You can always come up with a question, always: career, family, intimacy, inner life, leisure life, spiritual life. That's a lot to talk about. That's a lot of life to talk about and look at and to share with your loved one.

Personal Sharing Sheet

1. If you assume that you have 100% of life energy, how would you divide this energy among the six life arenas according to the way you live your life right now? Do you see where you might like to make some changes?

   a. Career   _____

   b. Family   _____

   c. Intimacy   _____

   d. Inner Life   _____

   e. Spiritual Life   _____

   f. Leisure   + _____

       TOTAL   100%

2. Do the same exercise you did in #1 above but, instead of using yourself, try to estimate the percentage of life energy in each of the life arenas for your aging parent. Do you see where some positive and meaningful changes can be made? How can you be of maximal help to your aging parent so he/she can make these changes?

   a. Career _____

   b. Family _____

   c. Intimacy _____

   d. Inner Life _____

   e. Spiritual Life _____

   f. Leisure +_____

       TOTAL   100%

3. How can you best help your aging parent to perform a life review? What props (picture albums, etc.) can you use? Where can you go to help him/her in their life review?

7

How to Deal
Confidently With Death

Not long ago the headlines of an article in a medical newspaper proclaimed: "Healthy families are the kiss of death for terminally ill patients." I was stunned. How can a healthy family be the kiss of death for the terminally ill? I read and reread the article and I still couldn't believe it. Researchers had studied patients who were life-supported by a kidney dialysis machine. Over a long period of time they noticed that some of these patients seemed to linger on and on, living longer than the rest. These patients knew they were terminal, that their condition was worsening, and that it was just a matter of time before death took them. But they fought off death and refused to die. There were others, however, who, after the diagnosis of this terminal phase, died very quickly. They simply signed out. The researchers wondered why this happened. All things being equal, there seemed to be something here which was creating short diers and long diers. They began to study this phenomenon. They found that the short diers were those people from "the healthiest families." I'm not talking physical health, but psychosocial health. That is, the patients in those families where there was open communication, where there was a feeling of well-being, where there was joy and delight and love being shown among the family members were the first people to die. This seemed incredible to me! It turned around all my thoughts on dying and family dynamics. I had always presumed that a healthy family would help to prolong life, would make a person stronger, more able to resist disease and death. How could it be that the people from "dysfunctional families," families where there wasn't a feeling of joy or a sense of togetherness, lived longer than the others?

Healthy Families and a Good Death

My line of work has been dedicated to trying to make families as healthy as possible and here they were dying on me. Why? Then the revelation! The "aha" moment came and it all made perfect sense. Those people who were from healthy families, who had a good sense of self-esteem and a good sense of well-being, knew that the family was going to carry on just fine after their death. They could perform the critical life-task of facing death and dying, and they could do this efficiently, effectively, and in peace. They were ready, their families were supportive, and the death experience was good. Death came swiftly for them. There is a point at which death treads lightly when it comes swiftly, and death came. In those families where there wasn't the same sort of health, where the person who was lying there dying felt, "How can they get along without me?" there was a sense of great uneasiness. Those were the people who went on and on, not for days or even weeks, but for months. They lingered and suffered all that time. I'm not suggesting that all people who linger therefore come from emotionally unhealthy families. I don't want that cause-effect relationship to be drawn. These research findings, however, do demonstrate that forces other than purely biological ones can have a great impact upon the timing of death.

Dying is likely to be the most stressful life-task that we have to go through. We have had a whole lifetime to prepare for it. We know it's coming; we know that our body will let us down someday. How we think of dying and death is extremely important. In that sense, death brings meaning to life.

The Stages of Dying

In 1969, Elizabeth Kubler-Ross first outlined her thoughts that dying patients went through five distinct stages before the actual death event. As adult children of aging parents, as caregivers, you should understand these stages. You need to recognize these stages and to conceive of them as natural and normal. In that way you can react calmly, caringly, and maintain your quality relationship to the end.

Denial

The first stage is called denial. In denial there is a conscious or unconscious refusal to believe that death is close. Not long ago I accompanied a physician to a patient's room when the physician had the unpleasant task of informing the patient, for the first time, that he had cancer in its advanced stages. The physician was very careful in choosing his words. Even so, I don't think the patient heard what the physician said. That was my impression because his response was, "Well, okay, fine." It was as if he wanted to push this information away and move to "more important" matters like what's for breakfast.

Kubler-Ross reminds us that denial is a healthy coping mechanism. It gives a person time to let this news percolate down through the system so that he can truly grasp that this is the beginning of the end. There is work to be done in the denial stage and we must allow it to be done. The length of the denial stage is usually rather short, usually from a couple of hours to a couple of weeks. Beyond this length the denial stage can become pathological.

Most of us are familiar with the flight or fight syndrome. When we are presented with an unpleasant stimulus, we either try to run away from it or we stand up and fight. The caveman standing at the opening to his cave sees a saber-toothed tiger coming at him. He has two choices. He can either run from it (flight), or he can pick up that big club and pound that cat over the head (fight). Denial of approaching death is flight, it's an attempt to get away.

Anger

When the defense mechanism of denial cannot be sustained any longer, the terminally ill patient moves to stage number two, that of anger. This time he uses his surge of adrenaline not for flight but to fight. In order to fight vigorously, we have to get angry. When boxers go into the ring and shake hands, there is not a lot of human kindness and compassion expressed. It is more like "I'm going to kill you, Rocky." They're building up anger. Their job is to attack each other and anger helps them do just that. This is similar to what happens in the anger stage of the dying process. The patient attacks death and consequently attacks anybody who's around. The doctor is attacked with such assertions as "He doesn't know what he's doing. He had no right to tell me that. He shouldn't have told me that I was terminal. He had no right to do that." Or conversely, "Why didn't he tell me sooner? He had no right to keep this information from me all this time." Or, "How do you think you would feel if you were in my position right now and you knew you were going to die?" These later questions are usually hurled at adult children. "How would you feel?" Or, "This is terrible. There is no justice in this world and there never was." These are statements of anger. You can almost palpably feel this huge rage filling everything in the room. It is just a tremendous amount of anger. And even though it is so extreme, it is normal under the circumstances. Anyone who deals in hospital settings sees this a lot. Then there's the ultimate anger, "How could God do this to me, if there is a God?"

What can you do in the face of such anger? "Dad, you shouldn't feel that way. This is not a good way to feel. God doesn't want you to feel that way." No! As you learned in Chapter Five, giving advice is usually not helpful. What is needed is to help that person express the anger . . . to get it out. Try not to dampen or impede it. Say that you understand why. "I'd be angry too. You have a perfect right to be angry. Go ahead, be as angry as you want. Come on, let's you and I both get angry together," might be helpful responses. Don't be fearful of the anger coming out; it's normal, it's natural, and your mother or father who is dying is not really angry at you, you're just a convenient target. Right up on your forehead there's a nice target, and if your parents are in that anger stage, let them hit the bull's-eye. That is OK because they need to get on with their dying. They need to get on with life and dying is their life right now. That seems paradoxical but that's exactly what's happening. They need to move on to the next stage.

Bargaining

Bargaining, says Elizabeth Kubler-Ross, is the third stage. Such statements as "God, if you take this cross from me, then I'll be the best person on this earth — just heal me. I want a miracle now. I've never asked you for a miracle before in my whole life and now I need one." Or, "Doc, look I know you do a lot of research around here. I'll be a guinea pig for anything. Whatever you've got I'll try it." Somehow the patients think that the physicians have some sort of magical cure, and they want it now. Here is an example of extreme bargaining, "How about deep-freezing me and then when a cure is found I can be thawed out, I'll come back to life, and they can cure me?"

Depression

When dying patients realize that all this bargaining will not work; when they realize the full impact of what's happening to them and they recognize that there is no escaping, then they usually go to step number four which is depression. Statements similar to "All that I have done is for nothing. I lived my whole life and I tried and I tried and look what it's come to" are common.

Another depressive reaction is for dying people to become almost mute. You can become very worried at that point because you recognize this is not a good way to die. You want to talk about this and could say, "I want to support you in this and it seems like you're pushing away." They say, "No, I don't need to talk! I'm not worth it. God has abandoned me so why not you? My health is gone; my body has abandoned me. So why talk about it? Besides, what can you do? What's the use?'' These kinds of statements are all typical in the depression stage. What they are actually doing is trying to get to the next stage which is acceptance. They are saying through this depression, ''I hurt because of the pain of the loss and the separation that I'm going to feel from you. I hurt emotionally and the only way I know how to express this hurt is to be depressed.'' Persons who were never especially good at communicating their feelings have a particularly hard time here. These are the kind of people that are going to suffer even more acutely because they lack the feelings vocabulary that was covered in Chapter Five.

Acceptance

Finally the last stage, the one you hope your parent achieves soon, is acceptance. Acceptance is that quiet and peaceful time of waiting. Statements like, ''I'm ready to go. I wish I would die. I wish that God would take me,'' and in its extreme forms, ''Won't you help me die?'' express this stage of acceptance very well. This can be a tough stage because there is something way back in your brain which is saying, ''Dad is suffering too much, perhaps the most caring thing I could do for him is to let him die.'' This stage is perhaps the most comforting for the patient but the most disconcerting for you. It's usually the one that lasts and lasts and seems to have no end. You then can have thoughts like ''Doesn't she love me?'' or ''I thought he was stronger than that!'' A sense of helplessness overcomes you as you think, ''What can I do?''

The best thing you can possibly do is to communicate to them that you are there. Just ''being there'' is important, along with using some of the skills that we have gone over about how to communicate. Focus on their feelings. You can also use life review to help them look back and say, ''My life has been meaningful.'' What greater statement could you make at the end of your life than that? ''My life has been meaningful'' is a most beautiful summation. Here is where the quality relationship that you've been working toward for so long pays such rich dividends. It's truly the jewel in the crown of your life with your parent. How loving a statement! The greatest fear that dying people have is that they will be alone, isolated, and in pain when they die. You can be there to assure them, "Mom (Dad), you will not be alone. You are going to die, but I'm going to be with you. The doctors are taking every precaution so you will not be in pain. I'm going to be with you. You are not going to be alone, you are not going to be isolated, you're not going to be rejected. I'm going to hold your hand; I'm going to touch your brow. I know you can't talk, but it's okay. I'm here."

Back and Forth

These stages are not permanent. The door to one stage doesn't close as another opens. People go back and forth; they can cycle back from one to another. Sometimes they move to the acceptance stage and then the next day you find them back in depression or anger or several different stages at once. It's easy for you to become confused because you don't know where they are. There doesn't seem to be a locked step progression from denial down through acceptance. You need to be aware that all these emotional reactions are normal and natural and, more than that, they're not your fault. Some of you have a destructive way of putting all the pain that your parents feel onto yourselves. You feel so responsible, like "I'm supposed to be doing something. I need to be doing something dramatic, if not heroic. I need to fly in that famous specialist from across the country and he will help my mother live." As the research on dying patients shows us, we are not always helping our parents in allowing them to linger. Dying is a necessary life task.

Response of the Family

We have looked at the stages the dying person goes through. Now we would like to focus on what happens to the family as they see their loved one dying.

Learning About the Illness

There seems to be five stages that the family experiences when one of its members is dying. Number one is the acquiring of knowledge about the sickness, accompanied by a certain numbness. The family members focus on the medical diagnosis. For example, your mom has been diagnosed as having cancer, so you go to the library and you take out books on cancer to learn as much as you can. You read books and articles and you get very intellectually involved with the topic. You become a quasi-expert on the subject and even start using the medical jargon to describe the changes she is experiencing. All this helps you to understand. However, this stage is also one of being intellectually aloof. You recognize that your mother is dying but there is not that gut feeling that it's really happening. You keep the reality of death emotionally out-of-reach.

Emotional Impact

Number two is emotional impact. It is in this stage when you start to recognize your feelings and become increasingly aware of them. It begins to dawn on you, "Hey, look. This is serious. Mom will not be around. She is going to die." The impact of the impending loss hits you. It's at this point that you begin to feel increasing levels of frustration and guilt. "Why didn't I do this? Why didn't I do that? I should have recognized what was happening sooner. What can I do now?" This is the stage, as painful as it is, where great emotional growth can take place because this is the stage where you are really understanding that death is imminent. It's going to happen. You begin to start looking at death in terms of what this death is going to mean to you. "What will happen to me as a result of this?" This is when you first start allowing yourself some tears. Growth is happening.

Depression

Then you move into the next stage which is your own depression. This is where you start your own questioning as to why this has to be happening. You make statements like, "Isn't it terrible!'' This is also called the "grow or go" stage, especially among close family members who deal with death. Some describe it in terms of being backed up against a wall. You have two choices, either you are going to grow with this death and continue to give help to this dying person, or you're going to leave in one way or another. Perhaps you will cut down on your number of visits to the sickroom. You will get involved in other things, start seeing more movies, reading more books, taking up your hobby with more intensity, etc. In one way or another, you will start avoiding your dying loved one. It's natural. It happens to some people. If and when this starts happening to you, understand it for what it is — depression. That's what is going on here. On the other hand, you may find this a time of commitment where you engage in the care of your family member even more. Jean's story is an enriching example of this.

Jean's mother was diagnosed with cancer two years ago. Jean was appalled that her father did not pitch in in a more active, direct way to care for his wife. He seemed somewhat distant and aloof; even rather cold and uncaring toward his wife of so many years. Jean was crestfallen at this, she was beside herself; she didn't know what to do.

For several months Jean came to a caregiver support group and related this dilemma that was so distressing to her. How could this man, whom she loved so dearly and admired for so long, become so seemingly callous overnight? How could he spend so much time over at the neighbor's house when his spouse needed him so much? These questions, and others like them, haunted Jean. She reacted in the heroic adult-child way; she moved in on the situation and began to attend to all her mother's needs.

As the weeks dragged into months, Jean began to wonder where her siblings were. Was she the only one who could or would answer this call to service to her mother, who had been the pillar of loyalty to her children for so many years? She felt alone, abandoned, and angry. She needed some relief. Jean always coordinated all the dealings with her mother's doctors, the hospital, etc. She handled it all. Her husband helped as much as he could. He was always there for Jean even if he didn't always understand her feelings. Indeed, sometimes Jean didn't understand her own feelings.

And then it happened, miracle of miracles. Jean took a step back. With the help of her friends in the support group, she decided that she would not be there when her mother was discharged from the hospital this time. She would let her father take care of that. The day came and Jean was beside herself with worry that her father could not or would not rise to the occasion. With great trepidation, Jean called her parents' home to find that not only had her father handled the arrangements with the hospital but that he was at her bedside caring for her. Indeed he had passed the test.

For the next three weeks Jean's mother went downhill. Through it all, her father was there — he nurtured his sick wife in the most caring and genuine way anyone ever could. The family gathered together for what was to be their last meal together. Two days later, Jean's mother died in her husband's arms and it was over. Jean came into the support group saying she had just experienced the most beautiful event in her life . . . the beautiful death of her mother. "You see," she said, "everything was complete, everything was right." One of God's little miracles.

Finding Hope

The next stage, number four, is emotional arrival. It is at this point when the depression begins to lift. The intense pain of the whole situation on you eases and you start allowing yourself the luxury of fortitude. You refuse to become overpowered by the feelings of pain and grief that are going through you. You say, "Okay, I can handle this. This is going to happen and I can handle it." In this stage you surmount the desperate emptiness of what death can sometimes feel like and begin to replace it with a sense of "rightness" if not actual hope that perhaps this death has a purpose and is more than a loss and, in fact, may be a gift.

Compassion

The last stage, number five, is termed deep compassion. This is a marvelous stage where your heart can swell with feelings of empowerment, of worth and value, strength and determination. Here is where you realize that this occurrence, this event that is about to take place, is not a loss but, in fact, a gain. You recognize the enriching qualities of the death and the meaning that is implicit in it. It's almost cause for celebration.

Not every family member is equipped to handle the dying process. Some family members are more comfortable with it than others and some simply are not emotionally equipped to be helpful or to experience the meaning at this point in their development. I pray that someday they do become more comfortable with death because someday they will face their own. The family needs to have compassion for all members and recognize that not every-body is capable of having a positive outcome to a family member's death. Allow the members who can shoulder the intensity the best to assume a family leadership role. Don't force anybody to participate or cajole, pressure or judge them to visit Mom seven days a week. Have compassion on them too.

Practical Suggestions

Here are some practical suggestions on how you can deal with all this. Some of these ideas we have talked about already. First of all, acquire as much information about the illness and the physical condition of your dying parent as possible. Get knowledgeable. If you understand aging and that dying and death are part of aging, then you have power to deal with it.

Secondly, find out how much your parent knows about this death process. Find out whether he or she knows the diagnosis as fully as possible. Many times in hospital intensive care units, older patients are heavily sedated and are comatose or they are delirious. In either state they know little of their diagnosis. Don't forget there is always some level of comprehension in the mind that looks so unresponsive. As much as you may think there isn't, you must assume they are aware at some level. Communication exists above and beyond the normal human levels of communication that we believe in. You can communicate through touch. Even if you think that the auditory canals are totally inoperative, you can still whisper, you can still talk, you can still communicate in your own way. Sometimes you can communicate by just sitting there with a person, allowing the vibrations that are in you to mold and meld with the vibrations that are in this dying person. Allow your body rhythms to mingle and to achieve synchronization.

Thirdly, break the conspiracy of silence. The conspiracy of silence refers to attempts by family members to "protect" the dying patient by keeping information from him or her. There are several variations. One is not to talk to Aunt Susie or Uncle Pete about the fact that death is approaching. You talk about everything else. "Gee, Aunt Susie, tomorrow is Valentine's Day. Did you get a Valentine's heart? It's so nice and warm here. Do you know that it's been awfully cold outside?" There's nothing wrong with this type of conversation if it's part of the total communication. If, on the other hand, it's the only communication you have with this dying patient, then something is wrong. You're not facing this person's death. The other variation of the conspiracy of silence issue is to say something like, "Don't worry about it, Uncle Pete, next week we are going to be out on the lake fishing. They are really jumping out there." This of course is denial. You are not dealing with death at all; you are talking about everything else. The third variation of the conspiracy of silence would be not to visit at all.

Fourthly, recognize what support is available for you and your family out there, not only prior to the death but also after the death. Many hospice programs now are developing and there is a whole new support system emerging that we've never had before in our culture. This hospice concept arose in England where they pioneered a much more enlightened view of dying and death than we enjoy in this country. They even assign counselors to the family to get the family together. "How are you reacting to the dying process? What kind of emotions are you feeling with regard to this impending loss?" I see this as healthy. You should become aware of these resources in your community.

We might wonder about support groups, "What am I going to get out of talking to other people who are going through the same thing I am? I know what I'm going through." Somehow, however, something almost magical happens within those support groups. If nothing else, these people will listen to you because they know what you're going through. Finally, don't be afraid to talk about religious or spiritual issues with your loved ones who are dying. Say prayers with them. Say the rosary with them. Watch services on TV. Read the Bible. Talk about it. Also, of course, try to control any pain and discomfort that's happening there.

Reactions After the Death

Now let's talk about reactions which occur after the death. We have words in our culture which we use to describe this post-death experience. The first one is bereavement, which Webster defines as the state or fact of being bereaved, that is, of being deprived, of experiencing a loss, especially the loss of a loved one by death. Grief is defined as a deep and poignant distress caused by bereavement, an acute sorrow, an intense mental anguish. The third post-death concept is mourning, which is to feel or express grief or sorrow, to show the customary signs of grief for a death.

Grieving depends a lot upon the personality of the one doing the grieving. Your style of grieving will be determined to a great degree by the way you have lived. It will also depend upon the relationship you shared with the one deceased. You are touched by every death you experience. You cannot not be touched.

Guilt

There are five natural feelings a grieving person commonly experiences. This is true of everyone at some level or degree. The first reaction is guilt. ''If only I had done more for Dad.'' ''If only I had not been so abrupt twenty-five years ago. If I hadn't married the man I did then my mother would really be proud of me.'' ''I didn't treat Dad right, I'm terrible, look at all the things I didn't do all his life and while he was dying.'' This guilt response includes a tendency to deify the deceased. ''He was such a great man. He did so much.'' Deification is a way of keeping your loved one alive in your mind and heart. Some people don't let their parents die. The ''ghost'' of that person lives on. ''This is the way Mother would have done it. If Mother were around we would be doing this today.

So let's do it." Mom's legacy continues to direct feelings and actions in the family as if Mom were still alive. A certain level of this in the form of traditions is healthy, but again moderation is the key.

Anger

The second response is anger. It's normal and natural to feel angry at this time. This anger might be directed toward the doctors, toward themselves, or toward other family members. There could be anger even toward God for taking this person. But the most curious anger of all is anger toward the person who died. Though indeed curious, it is nonetheless very common. I can't tell you how many grieving persons have come in to me and said, "I don't know why I'm feeling this way but I'm really angry at my father for dying. He shouldn't have died." I understand their feelings because I'll confess to you that I have some of those feelings within myself about my own father. My father died relatively young, at age fifty-seven. When I look at my own children and my own life, I say, "Why isn't he around so he could see me now?" I was merely out of my adolescence when he died; now that I'm a man I so wish I could talk with him, share my life with him . . . and, of course, that's impossible. I've even had the thought, "He had no right to leave when he did . . . his job wasn't finished!" I know he had no control over it but he is not here today and I'm angry about that because I want him to be here today.

Depression

The third response is depression. You begin to feel that there is no reason for living without this person. You experience a lack of energy, a kind of listlessness, lethargy, difficulty in sleeping or eating. Again, this is normal and natural. One of the things I counsel the physicians I train not to do is to give psychoactive drugs after a death, at least not for six months. I ask them to allow at least six months to go by before they start giving any kind of anti-anxiety agents, antidepressants or any mood-altering drug. The grieving process is much too important to be buffered by drugs; we don't want to take the bereaving, grieving process away from anyone because there is meaning in it and they need to experience it. If the grieving process is skipped or curtailed, it doesn't just go away, it simmers within us until something triggers it. At this point, and it may be twenty years later, you could experience an emotional reaction of guilt, depression, or anger very much beyond what would be considered normal for that event.

This brings to mind a woman who was very close to her mother. Her mother had been admitted to the hospital nineteen times in three years. Perhaps because of this, the daughter didn't entertain the possibility that one of those times her mother would not come out. But it happened; her mother died. The daughter wasn't able to be at the bedside. In fact, just then there was a huge snowstorm; the wake and funeral had to be put off. Somehow during that storm when this woman was cooped-up and literally couldn't get out of her house, she entered the stage of denial. She came back to the hospital saying, ''My mother never did die. You are holding her hostage someplace here in the hospital.'' After much counseling, she eventually stopped crying herself to sleep each night; that was after about two years. She is still grieving, however, and probably always will.

Tension

Reaction number four is tension and restlessness. I was in the service when my father died; I came back from Germany to attend his funeral. Then I went back to Germany for about another year and a half and then I came home. When I arrived in America, I found my mother very depressed and very anxious. She was frightened. She would place a chair up to the doorknob inside her bedroom at night for fear that something bad would happen to her. She was feeling so vulnerable that she wanted to put spotlights all over the outside of her house. She was feeling great tension and restlessness and as much as it hurt me to see her this way, I realized that it was normal. At first I felt helpless. I tried to deal with her logically by asserting that she was safe. I tried to reassure her, but to no avail. My only recourse was to take a very large risk. I explained to her that another family needed the house and that it was really time to move. Even though she could have lived more economically in the family homestead, we opted to enter a condominium community. With crossed fingers and a gulp, we signed the papers. She settled in so well that she lived eleven good years there until her death. The "significant emotional event" of this move seemed to stimulate her independence enough to allow her to take the next development step in resolving her husband's death.

Preoccupation

The fifth common grieving reaction is preoccupation with the deceased. This comes in many forms, none of which can be discounted. Dreaming is the most common form. "I dreamed about your mother last night and it was so real. I really saw her and she was in her favorite dress. We were at a picnic and Aunt Tilly was there and Uncle Steve was there. The whole family was there. We were having a great time." Dreams can be very therapeutic. Each dream is actually an attempt to resolve a life conflict. Dreaming does not indicate a morbidity. Actually it's quite the opposite. Dreaming is an attempt to make something that's confusing to you more understandable. Even nightmares have this purpose. If you have a recurring dream, try to discern the theme of the dream. It is trying to tell you something.

The second form preoccupation can take is to experience some minimal illusions or delusions. Your mother exclaims to you, "Do you know what happened? Your father was here last night." "Mom, that's ridiculous. Dad has been gone for five years." "No, he was here and I talked to him. He was so gentle and so kind and he had this radiant look about him." You needn't be overly concerned with such behavior. Unless they are excessive, these minimal delusions are not indicative of illness. Not long ago, I heard this story from a thirty-five-year-old man. "I went to our yearly family reunion. We were all there and I looked over at my brother-in-law and he had this strangest look on his face. I was feeling like there was a hand on my shoulder and I said to him, "Bill, did you just have the funny feeling that Grandpa George was just here?" "Yes I did." Grandpa George has been dead for seven years! Such experiences are more cause for celebration than alarm.

Stages of Bereavement

While the above mentioned reactions are the common responses to grieving, they needn't occur in any particular order. But these next four stages of bereavement are, in fact, sequential.

Numbness

The first one is numbness. During the first few hours or days after the death, shock is the norm. Beyond the feeling that you can't handle this, you might display little or no emotion. This is a time when it's very difficult to communicate. There is a term called "bereavement overload." This frequently happens to older persons when there is a succession of deaths among their friends or acquaintances. As more and more pass on, there seems to develop a kind of numbness which is hard to describe. It seems like another one passes on before the grieving for the first one has been completed. One overlaps the other. People who experience this become overwhelmed with grief and, as a consequence, they become numb. They are victims of bereavement overload. Talk to your parent about that. "How does it feel to have lost six of your friends in the last eighteen months?" When you hear statements like, "The old bridge group, there are only two of us left now," you can be sure that bereavement overload is at work.

Pining

The second stage is pining. Those who have suffered the loss of a loved one often react with a painful yearning when reminded of the deceased. Just about anything can remind them of the deceased: objects, "Your mother loved this painting"; places, "You are really feeling grief all over again when you come back here"; television programs, "Gee, Mom loved this program. You know I was with her so much when she watched this program." Adult children sometimes try to buffer this pain in many ways. They encourage the survivor to take trips. They reason that because their mother just lost Dad, this is a good time to take that Caribbean cruise she has been wanting for a long time. No it's not, it's much too soon. It is not the time to make big changes. For six or eight months after a death, try to keep everything in place. Allow her to grieve by encouraging her not to change, because if anything new intervenes in her life, you are sowing the seeds of unresolved grief down the line. You would be cutting her off from the opportunity to grieve and she needs to do it. Apply the same treatment to yourself. You also are grieving.

Dejection

The third stage is dejection, a feeling of hopelessness; lack of purpose and direction, signs of depression. As we mentioned earlier, the intense feelings of pain are decreasing at this point. These were the ones felt in stage two, pining. A sense of ennui or a malaise, similar to the unresolved grief outlined above, is felt in this third stage.

Recovery

Next is recovery. Here the survivor is beginning to regain interest in life. If you are that survivor, you begin to feel for the first time that there may be a kind of new life out there that can be enjoyed apart from the person who is deceased. Though your love has not lessened in the least, and the gap will never be filled, you have begun to live again. You are rediscovering and enjoying your surroundings once more.

Bereavement is a suspension of certain aspects of living which are necessary so that you can do the job you need to do. Now you, as survivor, can recycle through earlier stages. You can move through the whole process. This needn't alarm you. Especially at anniversaries, birthdays, holidays, and the like, the memories of years past will come flooding in again. You can again feel the loss, the emptiness, the vacuum is there. That's OK. My father died on Christmas day. Every Christmas day I feel him there. I'm sure that every Christmas my entire life I'll remember him.

How to Help the Bereaved

People are often just as uncomfortable with a grieving person as they are with someone who is dying. When you have grieved in the past you might have wondered why some people may not have come around to visit you. It's because they are afraid of death; their own death. You've just gone through it and they know if they talk to you that they've got to talk about death; at least they feel that they should. So they stay away. Is it you they are staying away from? No, it's their own fear of death that they are trying to escape. You have heard the story about the widow who, during the wake and the funeral, was just wonderful. She handled it all with calm and ease. Then when everybody went home, after the hubbub of the wake and the funeral was over, she collapsed. That's the time to go help the bereaved person the most. What they need the most is for you just to "be there!" Don't feel the need to fill up the silence. At this point, perhaps more than any other, silence is golden. You don't need to go on about the weather or Uncle Charlie's arthritis or anything else. Just be there. What you are saying is, "I know you are in pain. I care about your pain and it's going to be all right. We are not going to abandon you because we love you."

Conclusion

In this chapter we have covered some basic and very important issues in dealing with your aging parents. We looked at the dying process, at death itself, and at the bereavement and grief that follows. We looked at the stages of dying and the stages of bereavement. We looked at them from the standpoint of the dying person, the aging parent, and from your own viewpoint, the adult-child caregiver. This information should be helpful to you.

It has been emphasized that these reactions are normal, natural, and necessary. With that in mind you can get on with the business of living again. People do not die of old age. They don't have a disease called old age and we don't need to shun them. Dying and death are as much a part of life as is birth. It gives meaning to life. Death is only a physical thing and those of us who believe that there is another new life which starts when this life ends are perhaps in the best situation, the best position to be able to understand the meaning of what death brings. All of us die a little when any of us dies. We are all connected. We are all part of each other.

Personal Sharing Sheet

1. What was your first encounter with death? Describe some of the circumstances . . . who was there? Was it a loving and caring atmosphere? How did you feel? frightened? puzzled? supported?

2. How did your family approach death and deal with it? How did your parents explain death and expose the event to the children?

Epilogue

I would like to close these chapters with a poem. This poem was found in the belongings of a deceased woman who spent her last years in a nursing home. They had no idea that she had written this poem.

What Do You See?

What do you see, nurses, what do you see?
Are you looking when you look at me?

A crabbed old woman not very wise,
uncertain of habit with far-away eyes,
who dribbles her food and makes no reply
when you say in a loud voice, I do wish you'd try.

Who seems not to notice things that you do
and forever is losing a stocking or shoe.
Who unresisting or not let's you do as you will
bathing and feeding the long day to fill.

Is that what you are thinking?

Is that what you see?
Then open your eyes, nurse, you're not looking at me.
I'll tell you who I am as I sit here so still;
As I do your bidding, as I eat at your will.

I'm a small child of ten with a father and mother,
brothers and sisters who love one another.
A young girl of sixteen who with wings on her feet
dreaming that soon now a lover she'll meet.

A bride soon at twenty my heart gives a leap
remembering the vows I promised to keep.
At twenty-five now I have young of my own
who need me to build a secure happy home.

A woman of thirty my young now grow fast,
bound to each other with ties that should last.
At forty my young sons have grown and are gone
but my man is beside me to see I don't mourn.

At fifty once more babies play round my knee,
again we know children, my loved one and me.
Dark days are upon me, my husband is dead.
I look to the future, I shudder with dread
for my young are all rearing young of their own
and I think of the years and the love that I've known.

I'm an old woman now and nature is cruel.
Tis her jest to make old age look like a fool.
The body it crumbles, grace and vigor depart.
There is now a stone where I once had a heart.

But inside this old carcass a young girl still dwells
and now and again my battered heart swells.
I remember the joys, I remember the pain.
I'm loving and living life over again.
I think of the years all too few, gone too fast
and accept the stark fact that nothing can last.

So open your eyes, nurses, open and see,
not a crabbed old woman,
Look closer, see me!

More helpful books from Liguori Publications

Reflections on Aging
A Spiritual Guide
by Leo E. Missinne, M.Afr.

This book points out that the older years can bring about an increasing closeness with God. It helps readers enrich their lives by reflecting upon aging as part of God's plan. *$3.95*

Helps for the Widowed
by Reverend Medard Laz

This is a book of comfort and consolation for widows and widowers. It points out that God is calling you not only to *accept* but also to anticipate — to pass through the painful time of grief and look toward the new life that God has called you to discover. *$2.50*

Inner Calm
A Christian Answer to Modern Stress
by Dr. Paul DeBlassie, III

Combines modern psychology with spirituality to help readers discover greater peace and joy through the centuries-old method of meditation known as the "Jesus Prayer." *$4.95*

How to Forgive Yourself and Others
Steps to Reconciliation
Reverend Eamon Tobin

This book presents a simple, effective plan of personal and interpersonal healing that begins with "wanting to really want to forgive." It helps readers heal their own wounds so they can renew ties with a loved one. *$1.50*

Order from your local bookstore or write to
Liguori Publications
Box 060, Liguori, MO 63057-9999
For faster service call toll-free (800) 325-9521, ext. 060,
8 a.m. to 4 p.m., Central time.
*(Please add $1.00 for postage and handling for
orders under $5.00; $1.50 for orders over $5.00.)*